THEotherAMERICA

Teen FATHERS

These and other titles are included in *The Other America* series:

THEotherAMERICA

Teen FATHERS

by
Gail B. Stewart

Photographs by
Theodore E. Roseen

Lucent Books, P.O. Box 289011, San Diego, CA 92198-9011

Cover design: Carl Franzen

Library of Congress Cataloging-in-Publication Data
Stewart, Gail, 1949–
    Teen fathers / by Gail B. Stewart; photographs by Theodore E. Roseen.
      p. cm. — (The Other America)
    Includes bibliographical references and index.
    Summary: First-person accounts with four young fathers from varied
backgrounds describe their different circumstances and how becoming a
teenage father has affected their lives.
    ISBN 1-56006-575-3 (permanent paper)
    1. Teenage fathers—United States—Interviews—Juvenile literature.
[1. Teenage fathers.] I. Roseen, Theodore E., 1975- . II. Series: Stewart, Gail,
1949–   Other America.
  HQ756.7.S74   1998
  306.874′2—dc21
                                             97–37903
                                                     CIP
                                                     AC

Printed in the U.S.A.
Copyright © 1998 by Lucent Books, Inc.
P.O. Box 289011, San Diego, CA 92198-9011

Contents

Foreword

O, YES,
I SAY IT PLAIN,
AMERICA NEVER WAS AMERICA TO ME.
AND YET I SWEAR THIS OATH—
AMERICA WILL BE!
LANGSTON HUGHES

Perhaps more than any other nation in the world, the United States represents an ideal to many people. The ideal of equality—of opportunity, of legal rights, of protection against discrimination and oppression. To a certain extent, this image has proven accurate. But beneath this ideal lies a less idealistic fact—many segments of our society do not feel included in this vision of America.

They are the outsiders—the homeless, the elderly, people with AIDS, teenage mothers, gang members, prisoners, and countless others. When politicians and the media discuss society's ills, the members of these groups are defined as what's wrong with America; they are the people who need fixing, who need help, or increasingly, who need to take more responsibility. And as these people become society's fix-it problem, they lose all identity as individuals and become part of an anonymous group. In the media and in our minds these groups are identified by condition—a disease, crime, morality, poverty. Their condition becomes their identity, and once this occurs, in the eyes of society, they lose their humanity.

The Other America series reveals the members of these groups as individuals. Through in-depth interviews, each person tells his or her unique story. At times these stories are painful, revealing individuals who are struggling to maintain their integrity, their humanity, their lives, in the face of fear, loss, and economic and spiritual hardship. At other times, their tales are exasperating,

6

demonstrating a litany of poor choices, shortsighted thinking, and self-gratification. Nevertheless, their identities remain distinct, their personalities diverse.

As we listen to the people of *The Other America* series describe their experiences they cease to be stereotypically defined and become tangible, individual. In the process, we may begin to understand more profoundly and think more critically about society's problems. When politicians debate, for example, whether the homeless problem is due to a poor economy or lack of initiative, it will help to read the words of the homeless. Perhaps then we can see the issue more clearly. The family who finds itself temporarily homeless because it has always been one paycheck from poverty is not the same as the mother of six who has been chronically chemically dependent. These people's circumstances are not all of one kind, and perhaps we, after all, are not so very different from them. Before we can act to solve the problems of the Other America, we must be willing to look down their path, to see their faces. And perhaps in doing so, we may find a piece of ourselves as well.

Introduction

THE FACTS ABOUT TEEN FATHERS

Tony is seventeen years old. He should be a junior in high school, but his frequent absences kept him from passing any of his sophomore classes this year. His girlfriend Tonya, fourteen, has just given birth to their child, a baby boy.

"I'm not really sure how involved I'm supposed to be," he says with a mixture of pride and embarrassment. "Tonya's mama don't want me around, and Tonya keeps changing her mind. First she says she wants to get married, then she tells me she thinks the baby will be better off without me. She says that her and her mama can raise the kid just fine.

"But the thing is," he continues, "is that I would like to be there for that child. I work in a theater downtown four nights a week, and I make a little money. I don't know how much child support is, but I want to do right, you know? So I want to help pay for the baby, for the diapers and stuff. I want to be there, too. Maybe not be married, but be a father—take care of him, go on walks and stuff. But right now, they don't want me around.

"See, that baby is half of me," he says. "And I don't want to just leave. But Tonya's mama, she said she's going to call the police on me if I keep coming around. She acts like I want to steal him or something. I just want to be around. My father left before I was even born, and I didn't like growing up without a father. I don't want that to be my son."

AN ALMOST INVISIBLE GROUP

Tony is one of hundreds of thousands of teenage boys who become fathers each year. The pregnancy is almost never planned by both participants (sometimes a teenage girl will stop using the pill without telling her boyfriend), and few of the boys are married at the time of conception—although marriage is sometimes viewed as a "solution" to the problem of a teenage pregnancy.

The number of teen births in the United States has increased dramatically in recent years. It is estimated that more than 1.3 million teenage girls will give birth in 1997, an average of more than thirty-five hundred a day. The rate of teen pregnancy in the United States is higher than that of any nation in the industrialized world. Although it should be noted that not all of the babies delivered by teen mothers are fathered by teen boys, experts state that the vast majority of these fathers are under twenty-one.

It is difficult to get reliable figures of the number of teenage boys who become fathers each year. Compared with teen moms, teenage fathers are a far less visible, less well-defined group. They themselves neither become pregnant nor give birth; they do not seek welfare benefits or financial assistance. Their names may or may not appear on official documents such as birth certificates. In the eyes of the government agencies that assist and support single mothers and their children, the fathers of these children are a virtual abstraction. Perhaps for that reason, opinion of teen fathers varies widely.

"Many people picture [a teenage father as] an irresponsible young man who has fathered multiple children with different mothers, then walked away from each without another thought," states teen pregnancy consultant Jeanne Warren Lindsay.

Other experts agree, but stress that the stereotype is definitely based on fact. "Teenage boys who father children *are* immature," says counselor Claude Olsen. "They are children themselves, just as the girls are. Statistically, teenage fathers *do not* remain in the relationship for long, and often the girl and her parents or even grandparents end up raising the child. It's wrong to look at one partner or the other as the one at fault. The important thing to remember is that this is not a civil rights issue. No value judgments are being made because of economic, racial, or cultural reasons. Pure and simple, these are children, without a sense of responsibility strong enough even to use birth control, or to make sure their girlfriends do. Why would we think they would—or could—make good fathers?"

This is not to say that no teenage boy *can* become a good father, or that no teenage girl *can* become a good mother. However, the simple desire to achieve this goal cannot by itself overcome serious obstacles. A large number of teenage fathers, or those who will soon become teenage fathers, are simply overwhelmed by many previously remote issues that suddenly hit home: how to support a baby and a girlfriend, how to find a job that pays enough money for that support, and what is involved in being a father in more than name.

NOT AS EASY AS IT USED TO BE

Although becoming a teenage father is nothing new in American society, in today's economy the financial odds are definitely against a teenage dad, and this could be one very important reason why so few teenage fathers can provide for a family.

In the 1960s and 1970s a teenage boy had a far easier time supporting a girlfriend (or wife) and baby. There were more job opportunities for teenagers who had to drop out of high school to work full-time.

"I had my first daughter when I was seventeen," remembers one Chicago auto dealer. "It was 1964, and believe it or not, it wasn't as big a deal as it would be for me now! I was working part-time as a mechanic for my uncle's garage. I was earning good money, too. So when Moira told me she was pregnant, I dropped out of my senior year of high school and got on at my uncle's full-time. Nowadays, I know how hard that would be. First of all, most of the jobs teenagers can get now are flipping burgers at McDonald's, or carrying grocery bags at the supermarket. They probably get minimum wage, and that's not enough for even the kid himself to live on!"

The statistics certainly support his statements. Between 1973 and 1993, the median weekly earnings of young men aged sixteen to twenty-four working full-time fell almost 30 percent. (Males twenty-five and over made less, too, but their earnings only fell 7 percent in the same time period.) Economists blame the phenomenon on an increase in the number of minimum-wage jobs and a decrease in the number and type of jobs that do not require a college degree. "There's a great deal of competition out there for such jobs," says one high school counselor. "While a young man who could do auto repair or plumbing could easily find work thirty years ago, today these jobs are extremely tough to find—and even then, they require licensing or trade school."

For many years assistance and support in cases of teenage pregnancy has come from government—at county, state, and federal levels—and has focused entirely on the mother and baby. Many programs have simply handed out money, such as AFDC (Aid to Families with Dependent Children); others have offered support in the form of vouchers that subsidize, in full or in part, child care, education, health care, or housing.

Critics of these programs point out that the moment the mother marries the father, she becomes ineligible for many types of aid—thus eliminating the incentive for a teenage mother to remain with the father of her child. The government, by its generosity toward a mother and her children, is actually discouraging two-parent households, say detractors.

It is not fair to blame the mother, says one counselor, for the benefits available to a single mom are difficult to refuse. One Houston woman he recently counseled had what is considered an average packet of benefits for a single mother of two small children:

"She was getting about $280 per month in AFDC, $300 per month [in] food stamps, Medicaid (no amount mentioned, but call it at least $100 per month—certainly the insurance for a woman and two kids would be that much), and she was about to get housing (say, $350 per month in Houston). This doesn't even count all the other little [benefits] that she can get as long as she's a single parent—fuel assistance, free job training, day care during the job training, supplemental social security—that all disappear if she marries. (Well, she might get to keep some of the food stamps and some of the AFDC, depending on his income. But she loses the housing even if he's unemployed.)"

AN INVOLVED FATHER?

Such realities lead many teenage parents to view the need to form a family as optional. And when, in the mid-1990s, Congress acted to "involve" fathers, it only required that teenage mothers identify the fathers of their babies so that the government can force back payment of child support. Those who cannot or do not pay up lose a driver's license or have their wages garnished (if they are employed).

Eighteen-year-old Tomas says truthfully that he wants to be involved as a father. However, he has no understanding of the financial burden of raising a child. "I don't want to sound like a bad guy here—I love my girlfriend; I love my little boy," he says. "But no way can we afford to live together like she's living now. She wants me to help, and I do. I gotta say honestly that I can give time and energy a lot easier than money, though. I don't make enough to pay the premiums on my car insurance, and I gotta do that. I give what I can, I really do, but it's not nearly enough as far as money. But I'm always willing to baby-sit if she wants a night off to be with her girlfriends, or to take the baby for the weekend. *That* I can do."

STEPS IN THE RIGHT DIRECTION

A handful of programs currently work with teen fathers to make them more responsible. Such programs are most often offered at local levels but are drawing increasing attention at the national level.

Some call for strengthening existing programs in schools that educate all teens to the realities of pregnancy if abstinence or birth control are not employed. Other programs, such as Fathers on Positive Track in Boston, are aimed at boys who have already become fathers, offering them counseling and education in child rearing. MELD (Minnesota Early Learning Design) for Young Dads, which has spread to ten other cities in the Midwest, reports some success; MELD classes educate fathers on topics ranging from birth control options to finding and keeping jobs that would support their new families to the correct way to bathe and diaper an infant.

Program staffers have found that almost 80 percent of the teenage dads they meet have had little or no contact with their own fathers and in general lack models in parenting their children. Even so, most are eager (although somewhat frightened) to establish a bond with their own children. One MELD worker says that one of the most often heard comments from teenage fathers is, "I want to be there for my kid because my father wasn't."

Experts suggest that a threefold strategy of decreasing the number of teen pregnancies, revising welfare policy for single mothers, and encouraging programs that support both parents may yield positive changes in the young families to come.

A MORE PERSONAL LOOK

The following chapters feature interviews with four teenage fathers. They vary significantly from one another in race, economic level, and family background.

Jason, nineteen, is the only one who has married the seventeen-year-old mother of his son. The young family lives with her grandmother, although Jason would like to find a place where they can be on their own. He loves his infant son, Tyler, but wishes he had waited to take on the responsibilities of fatherhood. Jason shares the duties of child rearing with his wife, Jessica, but admits to being "exhausted most of the time."

Jamie, sixteen, is a high school junior whose daughter is a year old. His fifteen-year-old girlfriend lives with the child almost twenty-five miles from where he and his mother live, and he does not yet have his driver's license. He tries to be very involved in the lives of his girlfriend and daughter, but between school and work finds it difficult to spend much time each day with them. He admits to getting very lonely without them, and says, "I worry about the three of us staying close. I don't want to end up not being with them in the future, but who knows?"

Brad, who is seventeen, explains that his girlfriend, Kim, had their baby (Jordan, four months) when she was just fourteen years old. He says now that the whole thing was probably a mistake. Although he confides that he would love to be more involved with his daughter, Kim and her parents have made it clear that he is not welcome around the baby: "I don't think I ever felt so bad as when [Kim] told me, 'I hate you and Jordan hates you, too.'"

William's main fear at age nineteen is that his past life of crime and drug and alcohol abuse will come back to haunt him, spoiling the life he has now with his twenty-year-old girlfriend, Cathy, and their son. "I fight this battle all the time, every day," he says. "I don't want to go back to dealing [drugs], but sometimes we're so poor—me and my girlfriend and the baby—I get tempted to just make a fast score and then stop." His adoration of his son, Damon, is evident, and he looks forward to a second baby—due in about three months.

Some of these stories—told in the boys' own words—are disturbing. It is difficult to hear details of some of their backgrounds, which include violence, abuse, and neglect. For some, the future seems to hold little promise and the odds seem to be against their success as fathers or husbands. All of the interviews, however, contain a glimmer of hope that these young men, part of the Other America, can become what they wish to become—"real" dads.

Jason

"I DON'T THINK IT'S NECESSARILY
THE AGE OF THE PARENTS THAT
MATTERS IN RAISING A CHILD."

Author's Note: Jason is a young-looking nineteen. He married his girl-friend, seventeen-year-old Jessica, when they found out she was pregnant. The circumstances of Jessica's pregnancy seem to involve poor choices—both by themselves, out of immaturity, and by grown-ups who should have known better. For instance, after a period of stormy relations be-tween Jason and his own parents that resulted in his leaving home, Jessica's grandmother allowed him to live in her basement with Jessica. As Jason says in the interview, "I thought it was pretty trusting of [her grandparents] to let me come here. I mean, Jessica and I weren't sleeping in the same room exactly, but we were sharing the downstairs—a big basement area." Soon afterward she became pregnant, confirming the naïveté of Jessica's grandparents' trust.

The two teens love their young son and feel that they can make their marriage work. It is obvious to an outsider, however, that although they have some very grown-up responsibilities to shoulder, they are still woe-fully immature. For instance, when Jessica suspected she was pregnant she first confided in one of Jason's friends—hoping that the friend would break the news to Jason. Learning to be candid and open with each other instead of relying on junior high school games of "he says, she says" will help their relationship grow and become stronger.

The house is a small one, in a slightly lower than middle-class neighborhood in the heart of the city. The paper sign taped on the storm door asks that visitors not ring the doorbell: "We don't want our dog Dusty to bark, because Tyler is sleeping now." Jason an-swers the knock quickly, and lets his visitors in.

The room is full of overstuffed furniture, framed photos on end tables, and a large television. There is a game show on, which Jason turns off. He calls into the kitchen, and a tall blond teenage girl comes out, carrying a baby.

"This is my wife, Jessica," says Jason, pointing to the girl. "And this is our baby, Tyler."

He motions for his visitors to sit down. "This is Jessica's grandmother's house—we're living with her for the time being."

"I Like Being a Dad"

Jason is nineteen, but could easily pass for sixteen. He seems pale, as though he has not had much sleep. He is wearing a Nautica baseball-style cap, and after taking the baby from Jessica, he sits down on a sofa near the window. The baby is wide awake,

Jason talks about life as a teen father while his wife, Jessica, holds their infant son, Tyler. The teens, ages nineteen and seventeen, respectively, married after discovering Jessica was pregnant.

wailing with hunger. He smiles quickly as Jason produces a milk-filled bottle.

"I like being a dad," says Jason. "The nights aren't so much fun, but I guess that doesn't last long—that's what we've read, anyway. Tyler goes to bed at 9:00, sometimes 10:00—and sometimes he doesn't go to bed at all. It all depends. It seems like lately, with his teething, he hasn't wanted to sleep for more than an hour at a time, then he's crying.

"He likes being picked up; he likes to play. He hasn't been colicky, like some babies are. If he has a nap during the day, he likes to be up at night. That just seems like common sense, though. The trick is not letting him sleep too long during the day."

Next to him, Jessica looks even younger. She is seventeen, and very shy. She seems nervous, as though without the baby in her arms she has nothing to do. Jason continues to talk about his son.

"He's been staying up lately, just talking to himself, babbling on and on. That's a really cool sound, I think. I mean, at first you hear the voice, and you think, oh no, he's going to start crying. But then it's like he's talking to himself, just like he's in there on the phone or something. It's fun to hear."

"THERE WAS LOTS OF CONFLICT"

Jason says that he never dreamed that at nineteen he'd have a wife and a baby. His life until a year and a half ago was pretty quiet, pretty confined.

"I had led a pretty sheltered life," he says. "No, actually that's not right—I'd led a *very* sheltered life. I was always shy, kept to myself. I had friends at school, but I just didn't socialize that much with them. I did stuff sometimes with the kids in my neighborhood.

"My parents sent me to a private school—a pretty pricey one. I was there on a scholarship, because we didn't have much money. I wouldn't say it was completely preppy; the kids weren't snobs or anything. But it seemed like I never had much in common with them. I never fit in anywhere. Other kids were always making plans to go to games, concerts, stuff like that. I just wanted to hang out, maybe go get a cup of coffee or something.

"One of the other things that made me keep to myself is my grades. I didn't do real great in school—I hadn't done well even back in grade school. I didn't like studying or doing homework.

That made it hard to fit in at my high school, because the kids are pretty smart there.

"So I was on my own a lot. My parents are very religious, and extremely conservative. They didn't understand why school was hard; when I got to be a sophomore and junior, we had lots of fights about that. They wanted to make my decisions for me all the time. They didn't like the ones I made on my own, I guess. What they wanted was for me to be their little five-year-old boy, and I didn't want to be. So there was lots of conflict between me and my parents."

MEETING JESSICA

Jason says that when he graduated from high school, he felt that he had earned some freedom.

"I went to movies, slept late in the mornings, hung out with people, just drove around in my little blue Neon. I was working in a grocery store—I'd been working there since I was sixteen. I had money, and I felt like spending it. I had always saved so much of it, but it felt kind of fun to buy clothes, go places, just have lots of money to buy things. I wanted to have some fun before making any decisions about my future.

"My parents weren't happy about that. They really wanted me to go to college, and they were really disappointed that I didn't want to go. But there was no way they could force me, so I just kept doing what I was doing. I met Jessica at that time, through a friend. Actually, this friend was going out with Jessica. And when they broke up, she and I started going out.

"I knew right away she was special," he remembers. "I hadn't gone out much in high school, since I was so shy. I'd never had a long relationship with anyone, so I couldn't compare her to anyone else I'd had in my life. But she seemed so warm, and interested in what I had to say about things. She had a great personality—just really nice. I don't know, I just knew I wanted to stay with her."

AN EVOLVING RELATIONSHIP

They did not immediately begin a sexual relationship, he says. They began as close friends, finding they enjoyed each other's company.

"I actually left home and moved in with her before we'd started sleeping together," he says. "She was living here, with her grandmother and grandfather. And I was at the point where I couldn't stand being at home anymore. So Jessica asked her grandmother if I could live here, just down in the basement. She'd had other friends—girls—living here before on and off, so her grandmother agreed. I said I would be glad to pay rent, buy my own groceries—it was that kind of a deal."

Jessica interrupts quietly, explaining, "See, I live here because my mom and I don't get along. Really, it wasn't so much her as it was her husband at the time. And my grandma and I always did,

Jason moved in with Jessica and her grandparents when his relationship with his parents became strained. Although the teens are now married and have a son, they continue to live with her grandparents out of financial necessity.

so she said I could move in here. My mom lives quite a ways from here; my dad lives somewhere south."

Jason adds, "I thought it was pretty trusting of them to let me come here. I mean, Jessica and I weren't sleeping in the same room exactly, but we were sharing the downstairs—a big basement area. I think her grandfather was a little less enthusiastic about things, but her grandma was great.

"I don't know exactly how our relationship changed, what made it change. But we started getting closer and closer, and then started having a lot deeper feelings about each other. And that led to— well, you know, sex."

GETTING PREGNANT

Why weren't they more careful about their sexual activity so that Jessica would not get pregnant? Jason nods, shoulders slumped a little, as though he's heard this question many times.

"We weren't real careful, I know. We've thought about that over and over. Mostly when we did use protection, it was me. I used condoms, but I know that one time, one of them broke. We figured out later that the math was right for that to have been the time she got pregnant.

"Anyway, that time the condom broke I was really worried. I thought about it for a long time. But Jessica didn't seemed to be worried. And then, her period came, so I wasn't worried anymore. But she told me that it was a real odd period, real light and kind of messed up. I wondered, did that mean she could still be pregnant?

"The next month, she was late. A week went by, then two. Then one morning she said that she was going to buy a test, you know, the kind you get at the drugstore. She'd taken one the month before—I didn't know about that until later—but that test was negative. But this one came out sort of positive. I say 'sort of' because the strip was supposed to turn pink, but it didn't come out the same color as on the box. It was a real light, light pink. So we still didn't know. And boy, was I worried then!"

Jason says that although he was frightened, he knew that whatever the outcome of the test, he would stay with Jessica.

"I found out later that Jessica had worried about me leaving her," he says emotionally. "Actually, when she took that first test I didn't know about, when she had that odd period? Well, she confided in

Despite his anxiety about fatherhood, Jason says he was determined to stay with Jessica and offer support. "I didn't want her to be afraid of my reaction the same time she was worrying about being pregnant," he recalls.

my friend Nick, and asked him to tell me. And then Nick told me that Jessica was real worried she was pregnant, and that she was afraid I would leave her.

"That made me feel terrible," he admits. "I know she'd gone out with other guys before me, and they'd kind of abandoned her—not for pregnancy or anything—this was the first time she'd been pregnant. But I didn't want her to be afraid about my reaction the same time she was worrying about being pregnant. That was too much for her to worry about. So I told Nick that I'd take care of it, that I'd let her know that I'd never leave."

FINANCIAL REGRETS

But even though Jason knew he would remain supportive, he was still more frightened than he had ever been before.

"I was really scared, almost shaking," he says. "I kept thinking about what Jessica and I had planned for ourselves, and how that was all getting turned upside down. See, back a month or two before, I had proposed to her. We didn't want to get married right away, so we decided to take it slow. We just knew we were going to be married someday.

"At the time we had met, she had dropped out of high school and was working at Walgreen's. She didn't like her job though, and when we started hanging around together, she quit. Boy, I think of the money I should have saved! It was just one big playtime, like I said. I had my savings account, and between paying the $200 a month to my mom for the car (it was in her name) and rent and all the fooling around, I was getting really broke.

"Instead of being more careful, or working more hours or something smart, I sold off a bunch of baseball cards that I'd collected, just to get cash. I'd been saving them since I was little, and I had some pretty valuable ones. And there I'd be, spending money faster than I could make it. I worked for a while cleaning carpets—a friend of mine got me a job doing that—but it wasn't the right thing for me. My car kept breaking down, and I wasn't making enough money to make it all worthwhile. So I quit that, too. When I think of all the money I was throwing around then, I get depressed. I wish I had most of it back now."

GOING TO THE CLINIC

A few days after buying a third home pregnancy test and getting equally confusing results, Jessica decided to make a doctor's appointment.

"We made the appointment at a different clinic than she usually went to," he says, "because we didn't want to have other people know our business. This friend of mine, John, came along with us. He was the one that had been going out with Jessica when I first met her. He's been a great friend, even though he was a little mad

After receiving confirmation that Jessica was pregnant with his child, Jason was struck with the recurring thought, "I'm not ready for this."

at first that I started going out with her. But he ended up being the best man at our wedding. Anyway, he came along.

"The two of us just walked around outside while Jessica was in with the doctor. We had a cigarette, just paced around while we were waiting. It was like in those old movies, where the husband is pacing back and forth waiting for the baby to be born. My heart was beating so fast, I was so scared!

"I couldn't tell anything when she finally came out. She didn't look any particular way—a real neutral, blank expression. I was kind of relieved at that, because I figured if she were pregnant, she'd be upset, or crying or something. I kept waiting for her to smile and say it was a false alarm. We went outside, and John finally asked her. I was too scared. And I heard her say 'positive' to him, and I felt horrible."

"WE BOTH CRIED"

Jason remembers that as soon as Jessica told John that she was pregnant, she began looking as frightened as he felt.

"I could tell she was real upset then. I kept thinking, I'm not ready for this, I'm not ready for this. And when we got back to her grandmother's house, we went down in the basement, and we both cried. We just cried, and after that, we talked.

"We knew we had to tell people in the family, and we started with her grandma. I was torn between wanting to tell people and wanting to keep it to ourselves. I guess I was really worried that her family was going to hate me. But her grandma wasn't angry—in fact, she was very understanding. She said that it wouldn't help to yell at us. She said, 'You two need support more than anything else.'"

It was not as easy to tell Jessica's grandfather. From the beginning he had been dubious about the living arrangements in the basement, and that is what made Jason feel bad.

"I felt like I'd proved him right," says Jason sadly. "It's like he was thinking the worst, and we convinced him that we wouldn't be doing that, and then we did exactly what he predicted. We told him while he was having breakfast the next day; he was so startled that he spilled coffee all over himself. He wasn't real mad, but he was more upset than Jessica's grandma, that's for sure."

"JESSICA'S MOM LIKES TO PLAY GAMES"

Jessica remembers that it was she alone who broke the news to her mother. She thought about how to do it, and decided that face-to-face was better than a phone call.

"I *did* think it was best to choose a neutral spot," she says, smiling. "I thought, well, she can't really blow up at me in front of strangers, so I asked her to meet me for lunch down near where she works.

"I was expecting her to be surprised, or shocked, or something. But she really wasn't. She *knew*. We had gone into the bathroom, and I'm like, 'Mom, there's something I have to tell you,' and she's saying, 'Can it wait?' I guess she had noticed that we weren't alone in there, that there was someone else in one of the stalls. Then we walked out of the bathroom and she said, 'It better not be that you're pregnant.' My jaw just dropped; I didn't understand how she could have known!"

Jason adds, "She wasn't mad at Jessica, and she wasn't mad at me. I called down to her office, just to find out what had happened, to see if Jessica had told her yet. I was going crazy at the house by myself, just thinking about it.

Jason watches as his infant son, Tyler, feeds from a bottle. Jason says that informing his family about Tyler's impending birth further widened the rift between him and his parents.

"Jessica's mom likes to play games. When I called, she said, 'Oh, Jason, we have to have a little talk.' I'm thinking, 'Does she know? What's going on?' And then her mom says, 'It seems like you've been doing some things down in the basement.' I'm just saying, 'Yeah, uh-huh.' I didn't know how much she knew, and I couldn't tell if she was mad or not. I didn't know what to say. Finally, she said something that made me realize that Jessica had told her, so I was relieved. So she was cool about the whole thing—in fact, I think she was kind of excited."

"I WASN'T EXPECTING MUCH JOY FROM THEM"

Jason says flatly that he was far less hopeful about his own parents' reaction to the news. They had been angry about his moving away from home in the first place, so there wasn't much chance that they would be thrilled about his being an expectant father.

"We'd been having lots of arguments," he remembers. "I hadn't been keeping any kind of relationship going with them since I'd moved out. I called them—oh, I don't know—just once in a while. I mostly talked to my dad; he wasn't as mad as my mom was. But I wasn't expecting much joy from them about the news.

"I did see them at Christmas. It was at my sister's house. I had told my sister already. In fact, by the time Christmas had come, I had told mostly everybody in my family except my parents. I had called my brother in Arizona, and had told my brother Jared, who's just three years younger than me. It was nice talking to my sister—we took a really long walk very late one night. We just talked about the options, about what was best. She was interested in my feelings more than she was about getting her opinion in.

"So my sister knew that there was tension between me and my mom, and she knew about Jessica's being pregnant. She made it real clear to my mom that I was coming, and that she didn't want any yelling or anything, since it was a family time. But my mom couldn't leave it—she waited until the end of the evening before starting the fight. She was mad I left, mad I wasn't even considering moving back home.

"That's why I knew it was going to be hard to tell them. My mom was so angry at me for things, that I knew she'd resent Jessica. Not because of anything Jessica did, just because my mom would see her as the reason for me moving out. I wanted to shield Jessica from my mother's anger."

ROCKY RELATIONS WITH HIS PARENTS

"Actually," says Jason, "my mom had never even met Jessica, except seeing her for just a minute or two when we came to their house to get my car one time. See, it was in my mom's name, and I was supposed to be making the payments to her. I'd missed a couple of payments, and she got angry. That, combined with me moving out, made her really furious. She took the car back! She wasn't sure exactly where I was living, but she finally found out. She found the car, and got my dad to drive it back to their house.

"When I found out what she'd done, I yelled at her, she yelled at me—it was ugly. I said some things that I wished I could take back. It was mean, but it was just the anger talking. But then, it was so hard not to be angry. She was treating me like a child. I wanted my car, and she wouldn't let me have it.

"I went over to get it a few days later; I told my dad on the phone that I was coming. He said that he didn't want to get in the middle. See, my dad is a lot older than my mom—he's like the age of most of my friends' grandpas. And so I think this fighting was hard on him because of his age. I respected that he wasn't taking sides; he didn't want to alienate either me or my mom.

"Anyway, we got a ride over to the house, and then I found out that she'd done something so it wouldn't start. It turned out that she'd taken out the spark plugs. Anyway, we had a fight, and me and Jessica ended up walking home. So that was the first time my mom ever saw Jessica, and at that point, I was saying that I never wanted to see my mom after that."

Jessica interrupts quietly. "I knew that it bothered Jason after a while though. I mean, he went so long without talking to his parents, I could tell he was homesick. He acted real quiet, like he was somebody else. So I made Jason call her finally."

Jason nods, remembering. He adjusts the nipple on Tyler's bottle, and resumes feeding him. The only sound in the room for a few minutes is the happy sucking noise Tyler makes as he drinks.

KEEPING THE SECRET

Jason and Jessica finally told his mother on his nineteenth birthday. Amazingly, they had kept the secret from her for six months. They were both shocked, however, to find out that she already knew.

"I guess she'd been confronting everyone in the family—my brother in Arizona, my sister, even Jared. They didn't say any-

26

thing, because they knew I'd asked them to not tell her. But she suspected it anyway—I guess from just observations. Like once she noticed that Jessica didn't take her coat off one time, or something. Little things that she noticed, that we were unaware we were even doing. Maybe we were trying to protect the secret so hard, that we were subconsciously giving it away. I don't know what else, maybe it was just her intuition that told her something was up.

"So Jessica and I went to my parents' house on my birthday. I was sort of trying to get a better relationship going with my mom. Ever since I'd had that big fight, I'd felt bad. When I called her on Easter like Jessica wanted me to, I just felt that I didn't want to throw my family away. It was too important, even though we weren't exactly getting along.

"So when we told her and my dad, they weren't really mad. I mean, I could tell she wasn't thrilled. She told me again how I was so young, and I didn't have my life together yet. She asked me how I could think about raising a child when I didn't even have an idea of my future."

OPTIONS

"A lot of the stuff she was asking me, Jessica and I had already talked about," says Jason. "We had already decided that we were going to keep the baby, raise it ourselves. For us, abortion wasn't even an option because neither one of us believes in it.

"Adoption was an option at first. Jessica thought about maybe giving up the baby to someone in her family, maybe her mom or someone else. Her aunt is in her middle thirties and can't have kids. That might have worked out. But deep down, we really, really wanted to keep the baby. And we told my parents about that, that we'd made some decisions already. We knew we were going to get married anyway, so moving that up wasn't a big deal for us.

"I tried not to let the talk get too negative, because I didn't want them to yell at Jessica. I mean, the whole thing was my fault as much as hers." He pauses a moment, and then changes his mind. "I take that back—I don't consider Tyler's being conceived as a fault; it's not a bad thing. It's just as much my decision as hers, so I wanted to keep the discussion with my parents as positive as I could. And I think it paid off, because things have gotten a little better since then. My mom even gave us back the car to have so

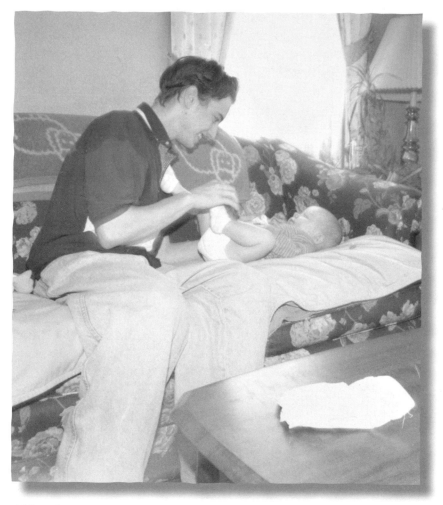

Although Jason and his wife share the responsiblity of caring for their young son, Jason admits, "I'm exhausted all the time, and I only do about half!"

we'd have quick transportation to the hospital when it was time for the baby to be born."

LOTS OF STRESS

During the remainder of the pregnancy, Jason and Jessica lived with her mother, although after Tyler was born, both teens were glad to move back to her grandmother's house.

"My mom had invited us there, I think, so that she could feel more a part of what was going on," says Jessica. "She was trying to make things easier for us, too. And Jason had a job at that time that was close to where my mom lives.

"But we moved back here after Tyler came. It was just too hard living with my mom. We had sort of a falling-out, more with my mother's boyfriend than with her. But it was unpleasant, and with a new baby, it just seemed like we should keep as much stress out of our lives as we could—there was a lot already, just with the baby!"

Jason adds, "The neighborhood over there wasn't the greatest, either. I had a gun pulled on me once when I was taking Dusty for a walk. Some car drove by, someone rolled down the window and pointed the gun. That's enough for me—I say, we don't need to be living here."

Now, he says, they've settled into a routine revolving around the baby. And while caring for the infant is not at all easy, it's at least fairly predictable. It helps a lot, they both agree, that they share the responsibilities.

"I'm not sure if it's exactly fifty-fifty," he smiles, "but we're pretty even on the time we put in with Tyler. I can't even imagine how a single mother can do it—I'm exhausted all the time, and I only do about half!"

A TYPICAL DAY

While they agree that no day is really typical, since there are always unpredictable changes in schedule, their days follow a pattern.

"For a workday, I get up whenever Tyler does," says Jason. "That's usually about 6 A.M. That's tough, because Jessica and I don't usually even get to bed before midnight or 1:00. We're still used to staying up late, like before Tyler was born. Anyway, Jessica isn't a morning person at all, so I get up with him at six, and change his diaper. He's usually hungry, so I feed him his bottle.

"I rock him, talk to him. Sometimes I sing songs. No, not lullabies—I don't even think I know any lullabies. I just sing stuff I've heard on the radio, and he likes that stuff a lot. I do that in the middle of the night, too, if he wakes up at 3:00 or 4:00. So after I wake up with him, sometimes he'll go back to sleep for a while. Sometimes I'll go back to bed, sometimes I'll just stay up.

"It's really amazing how a baby can change your sleeping habits," he says. "It's funny now. I used to be able to sleep through a tornado. I'd never hear alarms, never hear anything. Now, I can't even sleep through the cat walking by the door! I think it's something that happens to you—maybe you get more protective or something when you have a kid."

About 2:30 in the afternoon Jason goes off to work. He's now working as a security guard at a large office building.

"I like it okay," he says. "Mostly I sit in the lobby and watch cameras. It can get boring. But I bring a book and read, or I'm allowed to use the computer. Anyway, I get home at 11:00 or a little after. Jessica stays up to wait for me. We watch television, or just sit and talk. I don't get a lot of sleep, but I don't feel deprived. It's okay, how things usually are."

"SO MUCH RESPONSIBILITY"

Jason says that he has gained a new understanding of responsibility since becoming the father of an infant.

"I think, boy, a kid is so much more responsibility than I would have believed before. A baby takes more responsibility than a marriage, that's for sure. I mean, our marriage is something we take seriously, but you don't have to wake up in the middle of the night and change diapers. No twenty-four-hour-a-day upkeep with a marriage. Tyler *definitely* is.

"I also understand more about the stories you read about people losing patience with a child and hurting him. I mean, sometimes when Tyler is fussy, and I don't really understand why he's being that way—I don't know—you can almost feel like he's doing his crying and whining to spite you. I mean, I know he's not, but if you're short on patience, you shouldn't be with a whiny baby.

"It makes me sick to read about the stuff people will do to little babies—shake them, hit them— but I can understand the frustration. Not sympathize with it, but understand it. But you know, there's something called restraint. If you have none of that, you should never be having kids. It's not the baby's fault; you can't take your frustration out on him."

Both Jason and Jessica feel that it has been important for them to get time to themselves once in a while.

"We're lucky we have my grandma," Jessica says. "She will watch Tyler for us for an evening sometimes when we go out. We might go to a movie, go out to eat, or even just take a walk. And sure, sometimes we take Tyler with us. He loves to go on stroller rides; he loves the car, too."

They have no car now, however. The car payments and insurance were simply too much, once Tyler arrived.

"We're lucky, because I can catch the bus to work," he says. "And I am looking into getting a cheap used car. Jessica's grandpa is a mechanic, and we're hoping he can find us a car that's reliable. It doesn't have to be beautiful, just so it works!

"Otherwise, we're pretty lucky now. We don't have to buy a lot for Tyler yet. He's still so small that he doesn't need lots of big toys. He likes things he can chew on, since he's teething, and those things are cheap, anyway. Clothes are expensive, but we've gotten

Jason tightens the knot of his tie while getting ready for work. On a typical workday he gets up with Tyler at 6 A.M. and begins the normal routine of changing Tyler's diaper, feeding him breakfast, and entertaining him before leaving for work at 2:30 P.M.

some of that stuff as presents. We're on the WIC [Women, Infants, and Children] program from the government—that's a federal program that provides baby formula for infants. That helps, too. I guess right now, diapers are our biggest expense for him."

PLANS

Jason knows that even though they are enjoying the time they have with Tyler, they have to be looking ahead, too.

"Jessica is going to get her GED [General Education Diploma], so she can qualify for better-paying jobs sometime," he explains. "She's really determined about that. And she just got a job at a pet

"I guess I'd like to have more kids someday," Jason says, "but I can't even imagine what it would be like for us to have another one now. . . . We've got more than enough to worry about as it is."

shop. It's just for a couple of mornings a week. I can be home with Tyler until she comes home, and then I go to work.

"I'm going to explore the security field, do more than I'm doing now. I've heard there are lots of opportunities for advancement, and I'd like to think about that. Maybe this will be a career, but I'm not sure yet. I'm thinking about trying college. I never was much of a student before, but I'm older now, and I've got a good reason to have a college education.

"As to where we're going to live, I don't know," he says, shaking his head. "We know it isn't practical or even right to stay here forever. I mean, Jessica's grandparents were good enough to let us stay here for a while, but it's a little house. For the two of them, and for us, with Tyler, it seems like we should get a place of our own. My brother offered to let us live with him in Arizona. Eric is easy to get along with, and I'm pretty sure things would work out real well there. It was nice of him, to give us another option. We'll have to see how it goes."

What about having more kids? Jessica pipes in, quickly, "Nope!" Jason looks surprised. "Oh, right," he taunts, "you know you can't walk by a little baby now without getting all emotional."

Jessica blushes. "I know, but I don't want to go through the pregnancy, the birth, all that stuff. I'd like to have a baby, but I don't want to *have* the baby, if you know what I mean. Everyone tells me, 'Oh, those little ones grow up so fast.' And they do—Tyler seems so big next to those newborns I see."

Jason smiles. "I guess I'd like to have more kids someday. But I can't even imagine what it would be like for us to have another one now. People do it, but I don't know how they do. We've got more than enough to worry about as it is."

"THEY DON'T WANT TO KNOW THIS STUFF"

Jason has been a little disappointed by the lack of enthusiasm he notes in his friends concerning Tyler's development.

"I don't have much in common anymore with my neighborhood friends, that's true," he says. "It's kind of hard, because they were always important to me, but we don't have much of anything to talk about now. They're mostly my age, but it's like we're from two different generations.

"Like, they're not interested that much in Tyler. They don't come out and say anything, but it's just that they look bored when I'll tell them about funny things Tyler does, or if he's getting a new tooth or something. I know that they think it's really strange that I'm a father now. I don't think they really know how to deal with it. Jessica's friends, too. I guess we've handled it this way—we just make a conscious effort not to talk that much about Tyler when we're out with those friends.

"It's hard to do," he admits sadly. "He's someone we have a lot of energy and everything invested in. He's our whole life now, and to just ignore that he exists when we're out seems . . . I don't know

Even though Jason is dedicated to his son, he admits that it is difficult to be the only father among his group of friends.

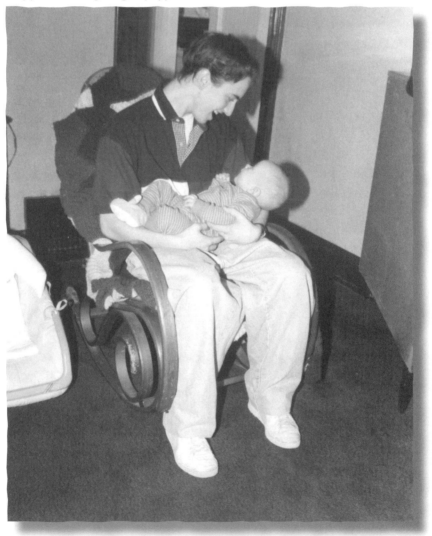

. . . disloyal or something. Like if I want to mention if he learned something new that day, Jessica and I have to stop and think, 'Oh, they don't want to know this stuff.' I guess that's just the way it will be until they have kids, too."

"WE STILL HAVE SOME THINGS TO WORK OUT"

How have his parents reacted to Tyler's birth? Are he and his mother on better terms? Jason thinks a moment and looks as though he can't give a good answer.

"I don't really know," he says. "I mean, I know they love Tyler. I know there's still a lot of resentment under the surface, though, stuff that still hasn't been settled between me and them. We still have some things to work out, me and my mom. I'm not as worried about it as I was before. I'm convinced that it's just a kind of mother-son thing. I mean, she had a vision of my life, of what she kind of expected that I'd do when I got older. And I haven't been measuring up to that vision at all. So she's disappointed, but I know that she'll get over it. I think—I hope—that as Jessica and Tyler and I are a strong family, my mom will see that I'm someone she can be proud of."

Jason says that he wants to remain close to his family, if for no other reason than to help his younger brother Jared.

"He's dealing with a lot of the same things I was at his age," says Jason. "He's kind of into his rebellion, he's been getting into a little trouble—staying out late, not letting anyone know where he is. There's a lot of stress between my parents and him right now. I've been through that, so I think it helps for me to talk to Jared. For sure, I'm the only one who can talk to him without backing him into a corner. I don't yell at him, and so he listens to me."

"IT'S DIFFERENT FOR A TEENAGE FATHER"

Has Jason received dirty looks from people who think he is far too young to have a child? He smiles.

"No, not really, but I know Jessica has. It's different for a teenage father. I think we might have it a lot easier as far as people making mean comments to us. People tend to be real judgmental and treat teenage mothers as though they were doing something really immoral. But as a father, I kind of get the opposite reaction. I think people figure that at least if we had a kid so early, I'm sticking around to do the right thing. Actually, most people I've run into seem cool about Tyler, but seem a little put off about me being married! I look young, I guess. But I try not to worry about other people's reactions.

"Besides, I don't think it's necessarily the age of the parents that matters in raising a child. I mean, my own father is really old. And he was a good father—I'm not saying anything negative. But to tell the truth, I missed not being able to play catch with my dad. Just about everyone I knew had younger dads who still had energy to do stuff, and I always envied them. Like, they'd go camping together, play sports. I wished it would be *my* dad that coached the soccer team, or *my* dad that could take us up to the Boundary Waters to go fishing. But with Tyler, I will be able to do all those things."

"I WANT TO BE HIS FRIEND"

Jason says that he tries not to hold too many preconceived ideas of what Tyler's life should be.

"I want him to test his own waters," he explains. "I don't want him to feel confined, like he can't even try something. If he makes mistakes, that's life. I sort of have a hope that he'll play soccer, like I did. I'm going to try not to pressure him into anything. I mean, if he likes sports, great. If it's music, or something else, great. I guess I'll try to keep the little soccer fantasy to myself—but it's kind of fun to think about. Maybe I'd coach his team when he's older.

"I think I'll be a strict father. I won't take a lot of crap from him. I want him to make his own decisions, as I wish my parents had let me. I led a very sheltered life, and I don't want that for him. I want him to be friends with a wide variety of people, hang out with lots of kinds of kids. I mean, he's a city boy—I'm not going to send him to some fancy private school if it limits him that way."

Is he happy his life has taken this direction? Jason looks tired.

"If I could give some advice—if anyone who's a teenager now would listen? I'd say, 'Wait.' I don't regret what happened, but I wish Tyler had happened later. I wish I was doing other stuff now, not having to be so responsible all the time. I think it's because I've gone from complete irresponsibility to complete responsibility, and that's been hard. I have no more freedom to come and go, to do things at the spur of the moment. It's real hard to get used to that feeling.

"I know my friends feel that I'm tied down now. I'm trying not to feel that way, because I don't want to resent my life. I love Jessica, I love Tyler. But being married with a child at nineteen—that's not a good idea. Financially, you'll be strapped. No car, no buying new clothes, no partying."

Jessica interrupts again. "I sometimes even wish for a few minutes that I was back in school being a cheerleader. That's what I'd be doing now, if it weren't for having Tyler. But I'm the same as Jason, I wouldn't trade him for anything."

Jason hoists Tyler to his shoulder and pats his back softly. "I just want people to know how hard it is, before you get involved. Be ready for a big, big change."

Jamie

"I DON'T WANT MY DAUGHTER TO START AS EARLY AS ME IN BEING A PARENT."

Author's Note: Jamie was introduced to me by a high school counselor, who said that although Jamie has had some difficulty at school, he was "a really good kid." He seems sweet tempered and soft-spoken, unexpected traits considering his gang background back in Gary, Indiana. He stresses that he is a changed person now, mostly because of his devout trust in God.

Like some of the other teens interviewed for this book, Jamie's vow to be there for his child seems in part a reaction to childhood abandonment by his own father. He says many times how happy he is to be a father, and how proud he is that he can provide for his new daughter. His youth and naïve ideas are evident when he describes his vision of his future education and career.

I caught up with Jamie in the high school weight room. He is a big African American kid, sixteen years old, who might have the body of a linebacker in a year or two.

He's working his lower body on a weight machine, and sweat is pouring from his forehead. Unlike some of the other boys using the equipment, Jamie has not changed from his school clothes. He is wearing old, no-name basketball shoes, a pair of worn blue sweatpants, and a gray sweatshirt.

"HEY, I DRESS LIKE A BUM!"

"I got a kid, yeah," says Jamie, wiping his brow with a paper towel. "She's a little girl, just turned one. Her name's Easha. And I think I'm a good father. Hey, I know one thing—I sure spend a lot

Jamie works out in the weight room of his high school. Jamie's girlfriend, Elishai, gave birth to their daughter, Easha, when Jamie was just fifteen years old.

on that child. I'm always buying her stuff. Hey, I dress like a bum! She's got better shoes than me, she's got little Jordans, little red-and-white ones. I got these old ones, I don't even know who makes 'em. But like I tell my mama, 'I'll go like a bum for my kids, I won't let them be without, not me.'

"I see her pretty much every day, except when I'm working," he continues. "She lives most of the time with my girlfriend, Elishai, about twenty-five miles north of here. I take the bus out there when I get home from school. I take a shower, change, then grab some money out of my drawer, or if I'm broke I ask my mom. It's a long bus ride, maybe an hour or more from my house. There's a transfer, and if it's rush hour, it takes a little longer. I wish I could take my mom's car. I know how to drive it, but she won't let me until I get my license.

"I meet them out at the mall near where Elishai lives, and we hang around there, just talking, having fun. If it's near a holiday or something, like maybe there's an Easter bunny, or Santa Claus or something, then I get her picture taken. Sometimes I buy her something—a toy, a new sleeper, a little shirt. She's got lots of things.

"Sometimes on weekends Easha comes to stay with my mama and me. I really look forward to that; I like playing with her. We play with her toys, just sit around the house or whatever, you know. Sometimes I let her sit on my dog's back. I make sure he don't bite her, though. He's pretty good—doesn't start jumping around or anything. And she likes it.

"Her toys? She likes Barney, and some dolls, and some little squishy toys for her bath that make noise when you squeeze them. She likes being held, and going out in the stroller. She's pretty easy to take care of. Every time I'm not sure about something, I ask my mama, 'cause she knows a lot about babies."

A LONG RELATIONSHIP

Jamie and his girlfriend Elishai have a good relationship, he says, partly because they've known each other a long time.

"We met more than two years ago," he says. "I was over at my auntie's house, and this man came over. He and my auntie have been friends for a long time. So he brings his daughter—that was Elishai—and my auntie's saying things like, 'Hey, James, see that, she ain't got no boyfriend.' And we got to talking a little bit that time, and I kind of liked her.

"I didn't start going out with her right away, though. Up till then, my auntie was like pressuring me about did I want a girl-friend, or whatever. And my brothers and sisters and everyone were talking for me to her. I got mad at that; I told them I could manage my own business.

"Well, she ended up making the first move. She called me and said, 'Jamie, you know if you want to talk to me, just come over and talk to me.' And so I said, 'Yeah, I will do that.' So then on December 23 it was my cousin's birthday party, and we were both there. I went over there where she was, and I brought some ice cream and cake over to her, and we started talking some more.

And after that, I don't know, we started going out sometimes, and getting to know each other better."

"I Liked Her a Lot Almost Right Away"

Jamie remembers feeling as though he and Elishai clicked right away.

"She was a nice person, really warm and friendly. She gets in her moods, just like I get in my moods, it's a back-and-forth thing. But we always seemed to fit real good. We went out, went to the movies. Sometimes we met downtown—it was kind of midway between her house and mine. We'd just hang out, go eat together. Sometimes we'd go back to her house.

"We didn't start having sex until after about two or three months. We talked about it and talked about it. We agreed that before we got too serious, we'd go downtown and have, you know, the AIDS test and stuff. I mean, we were fourteen then—she didn't know who I'd been with before, and I didn't know who she'd been with before. It was just the logical thing. I mean, we'd both had relationships before, yeah. It ended up that we were both negative, so everything was fine."

What about birth control—who was responsible for that? Jamie shakes his head.

"We was having sex at first—we didn't talk about that at all. After she had the baby, then her mom said she should get on something so this doesn't happen again. We didn't want to have more kids yet, she said. So no, we weren't really thinking about it. I mean, I usually carry a condom with me, have it in my wallet. I know about protection. But they can break a lot."

Jamie's voice trails off. He has walked over to the mat to do push-ups.

"Wishful Thinking"

The idea of Elishai getting pregnant didn't seem very real to them at first. They were enjoying each other, and having fun, says James.

"It isn't very hard finding places to have sex, even if you're still in high school," he says. "We didn't do it at my house, no. But we'd go to her sister, and have her get us a hotel room. Or we'd go to a friend's house if no parents are home. Sometimes we went to a little party—kids would say, 'Come on over, we're having a little house party; our parents aren't home and you can do

Jamie and his girlfriend were both fourteen when they started having unprotected sex. When they learned that Elishai was pregnant, Jamie says there was never a doubt that they would keep the baby.

whatever you want.' We'd do that, yeah, just go back to one of the rooms or whatever.

"In fact," he remembers, "that was how we had sex the first time, at one of those parties. We were having fun, playing a little spin the bottle, you know. And one thing led to another, and then we were upstairs. Things went on, you know, from there."

After about four months, Elishai came down with what she thought was a virus of some sort.

"We were real scared," says Jamie, "because we thought she had some kind of disease or something. Lots of throwing up, even in the middle of the night. She did seem kind of bloated around her middle, and I asked her, 'Why's your stomach getting so big?' She just thought she was bloated up from her period coming, or maybe from the virus or something.

"My mama was the one who suspected it. She came with us to the clinic, mostly because she knew I was really worried about what was wrong with Elishai. She was there, kind of supporting us, you know? Even when she'd say that maybe it wasn't a virus, that it could be Elishai was pregnant, I thought she was just hoping for another grandkid. See, my older brother and me are the only two kids in our family that haven't had kids. And he's eighteen, so everyone thought he would be first before me. So we kind of figured it was wishful thinking on her part."

"Never a Doubt"

According to Jamie, he was very proud when the doctor at the clinic announced that Elishai was pregnant. He admits, however, that there was a little nervousness mixed in with that pride.

"Yeah, I was a little scared, for a minute," he laughs. "I was so proud, though! I kept thinking, I've helped create a baby! The scared part was in telling her mom, that she might be mad at me and not want me around no more. Elishai was scared of that, too—in fact, she was going to try to wait until she was seven or eight months along before she told her mother.

"But it was okay how it worked out. We had a meeting—her mom, my mom, me, and her. We sat down and talked about it. Her mom was surprised—but she was like my mom. They were both saying, 'You all made a baby now, so show some responsibility.' Mostly I was so relieved that Elishai's mom didn't stop liking me. I mean, her mom's always been so great—I call her 'Mom' just like Elishai calls my mom 'Mom.' She thinks of me as her son, and that's cool. I'm really close to her—and Elishai's father, too."

Asked whether their decision to have the baby, and to keep it, was ever in doubt, James shakes his head vigorously.

"Never a doubt, never a doubt," he states. "We didn't consider abortion. We both wondered why we would think about killing a baby that God let us create, you know. That wasn't right at all, and we couldn't have lived with ourselves if we'd done that. And since we would have the baby, it just made sense to keep it. We both thought that; we were really strong on that."

Jamie is determined to take responsibility for his new family and to remain a prominent figure in his daughter's life.

"THE RESPONSIBILITY IS ON ME"

Jamie has finished his workout. He stands up and grabs a handful of paper towels, drying his face and neck. He smiles, and puts his thumb on his chest.

"See, the thing you don't know about me is this: The way I got to look at everything—the responsibility is on me. We didn't set out to have no baby; it just turned out that way. And a lot of kids my age that get their girlfriends pregnant, they get a lot of disrespect because that's the way they treat their girlfriends. Once they hear that she's pregnant, they take off, or else they just say to her, 'You can't prove that's my kid.' But that's not me. See, my dad took off, he left us when I was just eight months old. I always listened to my mama—she says that if you get a girl pregnant, you stay there for her. I didn't want to be like my dad was for me. I been there the whole time for Elishai, and I'm there now."

Jamie says that her being pregnant and giving birth has not diminished the way he feels about his girlfriend.

"If anything, I feel a lot more, a lot more," he says warmly. "I know we've talked about getting married soon, as soon as we both turn eighteen. Until then, I'm going to look for an apartment after next year, and then we can be together until then. Our family of three—that's nice, yeah. We'll be living on our own, not sharing no place with our mothers.

"As things are now, I'm going to school and so is she. I'm going to be a junior next year; she's going to be a sophomore. The baby goes to day care during the day. Every other weekend or so my mama and I have Easha for the weekend and give Elishai and her mama a break. That's only fair—plus my mama really enjoys having that baby around."

"I WAS SO HAPPY, I CRIED"

After a fairly routine pregnancy, Elishai gave birth to a little girl. It was an experience Jamie says he will remember for the rest of his life.

"When it was getting time for that baby to be born, her dad was real upset and nervous. He wanted to get out of there, didn't like being around it all. He told me, 'Come on, we'll go out on the town, buy some cigars and stuff, have us a party and celebrate.' But I told him, 'But I want to see my child being born—I want to stay here.' I went with him, though, just for a minute. We went out and bought stuff, had a little party, and I was really happy.

"When the baby was born, well, I can't tell you how it made me feel. I was so happy, I cried. I went downstairs in the hospital and bought a whole big bunch of balloons. They all said IT'S A GIRL! I felt so proud, seeing that baby. She's so pretty—she's like a little doll. Sometimes I would look at her when she was first born and think, 'Man, she doesn't even look real.'

"We knew right away what her name was going to be; the name Easha was Elishai's mom's idea. It's just a name—it doesn't mean anything, or come from anyone else like a great-grandma or anything. It's just a name she liked because of how it sounded."

Jamie looks blank when asked the day of his daughter's birthday. "I can't think of it right offhand," he shrugs, smiling. "My mom would know it. I think it's in July or something.

"But," he warns, "don't think that just 'cause I can't think of the date, I'm not a good father, because I am. I mean, everybody was telling me almost right away how good I was with that baby. She'd settle right down if she was crying as soon as I held her. And I knew what to do—like feeding her, holding her, putting on diapers. My mom told me, 'James, you're going to be a real good father,' and that made me feel real good."

COMING FROM GARY

Jamie is adamant about the importance of his mother in his own life. Growing up without a father, he says, put extra pressure on his mother to see that her family didn't get into trouble.

"She's a strong woman," he says proudly. "She moved my family—all my brothers and sisters—from Gary, Indiana, to here. She wanted it, because she said that place wasn't a good environment. Lots of fighting, lots of crime. I was thirteen then, the youngest of all the kids. Me and my brother had gotten kicked out of our school for fighting. Yeah, it was permanent, I think, it was like we was expelled.

"It wasn't no gang thing. It was just a dispute with someone, and then it got real ugly. Me and my brother were helping each other fight, and that's what happened. To tell the truth, though, I *did* hang out with gang kids back in Gary, although I wasn't in a gang. I'd be everybody's friend—I hung with the Lords, the Stones, the GDs, all them gangs in Gary. I hang with my brothers, my sisters' boyfriends, friends who were in gangs. I didn't want to get myself beat up or shot at, so that's why I chose not to be in a gang.

"I carried a gun all the time except going to school. I never carried no knife or anything else. It was just that kind of place. Plus, I did sell drugs, although I ain't proud of that now, sitting here. I never used no drugs, but I sold crack, mostly. When my mama decided to move here, I left my gun back there. My brother told me I was a fool to leave it, especially if I was going to be selling here, too.

But I wasn't sure how much I was going to be selling, so I left the gun—actually the *guns*, since I had a bunch of them. Besides, when my brother left here and went back to Gary, he told me that if I ever wanted a gun, I'd just say the word and he'd send me one."

GETTING RELIGION

Jamie credits his mother with making him religious, too. Back in Gary, he didn't have any interest in going to church with her.

"I wanted to sleep late," he admits. "I was not a religious person, because I figured the church was no place for me. But when we came here to live, she asked me to come with her. I don't know why I told her I would—I think she was more insistent than usual. I'm not sure. But it was an experience that changed my life.

Jamie says his mother (pictured) is an important and influential person in his life. In addition to helping stabilize his homelife, she has been a loving grandmother to Easha.

"I'm sitting in church, right? And all of a sudden I'm hearing voices saying, 'All drugs is doing is killing human beings.' And I'm completely scared! It was God, not a person. It was like a voice that was inside me that was real. It told me that I should throw the drugs that I had away, as soon as I got home.

"After church was over and we went home, I ran to my room and got those drugs out of my drawer and threw it all down the toilet. I did that, and I swear to you, I ain't never touched drugs since. I

Jamie and a friend share a joke while sitting on the steps to his house. Jamie says he has little time to socialize with friends outside of school. "My after-school time is work, my girlfriend, and my daughter," he says.

haven't even been around them. I don't want to be part of that killing the voice was talking about. I don't want to be a father, telling people that's what I do for a living—selling crack. That's not good.

"Your actions, you know, they go a long way, and you don't know when you're doing something like selling to a kid—maybe he's going to go off on his girlfriend or murder some guy. That's my fault then, too, 'cause I put those drugs in his hand so he could take them. So it's blood money I make, and I don't want blood money. See, when I spend $200 on my daughter, like I did last Saturday buying her clothes and stuff, I don't want to be thinking that's blood money. That's wrong.

"Hey," he smiles, "one time at church, and that did it for me— I'm grateful to my mama that she made me go. I go back now, regular each Sunday. I even sing in the choir with my girlfriend, and I never thought I'd do that! We're even working on raising money for a trip next year, a celebration trip for our church choir. We both want to go on that, so hopefully we'll all raise that money we need—but it won't be from selling no drugs!"

"It Was Like a Sign or Something"

Jamie is convinced that there are some things that are just meant to happen. His daughter's birth, his revelation at church—those are like signs, he says, to teach him something.

"But there is one other thing that happened that I think is meant to keep us smart about Easha, about how we raise her. I was watching a scary movie on television. I was sitting there with my girlfriend and Easha—they were asleep, just dozing. And I'm not really concentrating on the movie, because I'm thinking about my brother in Gary, how he'd gotten shot. It really made me upset, you know, and I couldn't stop thinking about it. And all of a sudden I'm seeing these black things crawling around the floor, crawling everywhere.

"I woke Elishai up, I'm saying, 'Do you see this? Look at this!' She told me she didn't see nothing, she didn't know what I was talking about. So the next day, I told my mama about it. I said that I was thinking about my brother and started seeing this stuff crawling around, crawling on me. I asked her did she know what it was or what it meant.

"Well, my mama told me to stop acting like a fool. She told me it was stupid to watch all these scary movies on TV—plus she said,

'Why are you having that stuff on while your baby is in the room—that can't be good for her. You can never tell what will give a baby bad dreams.'

"So now, the only thing I watch on TV is cartoons. I don't know, maybe it was a sign or something. It's really a good thing it happened with me seeing that stuff crawling around—kind of a combination of real stuff and made-up scary things. It reminded me

Jamie and his nephew pose for a photograph. Now that he has a child of his own, Jamie worries about harmful influences, such as scary movies, affecting his daughter.

about taking good care of my daughter, so she doesn't see that stuff and get frightened. It helps me protect her."

"I'M IN UPPER MATH NOW"

As Jamie leads his visitors down the school hallway, he greets the teachers he passes. He admits that he has not been the model student, but says that he has been working hard lately.

"I got suspended last Friday because my math teach said I called her the 'b' word," he says disgustedly. "I didn't do no such thing. I don't know what I said, but it wasn't that. But if they think you did it, you did it. That's how it is around here. The principal just sends you home, and you can't come back until you miss a day of school.

"My biggest problems in school are with reading and English. And science," he adds. "I don't do so good in that. My reading isn't so good, and I know I go too slow—I can't keep up with my English class when we read stories. I'm not doing too great in science or health right now, I know that. But math I do real good. I'm in upper math now, and I score higher than most of the twelfth graders at my school, so that's real good. I think it's hereditary or whatever, because my mama told me that lots of people in our family are real good at math, too."

Jamie says that playing football has made school more fun this year.

"I made the JV team," he says, "and next year I'll be on varsity. I'm working out, like you saw, doing weights after school or during my study period. That's good for me, good for my upper and lower body. It's going to help me a lot next season, see, because I play on the line, and you got to be really in shape or you're going to get beat every play. Plus I got to know more of the guys, and it's nice when you got friends at school. Even though I do know some people, though, I don't hang much with them at all. Just at lunch or whatever—my after-school time is work, my girlfriend, and my daughter."

THINKING ABOUT HIS FUTURE

It's clear that Jamie is taking his role as a father seriously. He says that he thinks a lot about the future now, something he never used to do.

"It's different now, real different," he says, looking a bit overwhelmed. "Running around like I used to do in Gary, I didn't think much about school, or working at anything except selling my drugs. That was the way I was making money. Now, working at the discount store three days a week—I don't make nearly the money, but I feel better about it. There's no carrying guns, no standing around with crack in your pocket. And except for a little bit, I bank most of my paycheck.

"School has this thing where they let me have part of my day for work, too. I take three classes, then I can leave. Before I did that, I had to take some classes at the job training center. That was helpful, because it taught us how to maintain a job, things like that. In a couple of weeks I'm going to start at another job, working as a janitor at my church! I'm looking forward to that as a part-time job.

"But I think a lot about how I can't do this forever," Jamie admits. "I'm going to be graduating school in a couple of years, and I want to get a real job. I'm going to be getting a lot more money, because when you pay rent, support a little family, you got to have a steady income. Plus, I want it to be something I like, so I won't always be thinking about getting a day off."

OPTIONS

Jamie says he isn't sure what field he will end up in, but is happy that he has some options.

"I think about being a carpenter someday," he says. "I like making things. Like, I made Easha a little sandbox out in the backyard, and she really loves it. I'd maybe go to a trade school to learn carpentry after I graduate. Maybe I'll end up owning my own business, building houses for people someday. I'm interested in that. My cousin—he said he could find me an application for a carpenter's college. He knows about that stuff, so I'll keep talking to him.

"Now, if you ask me how I see myself at thirty years old," he says uncertainly, "I'm kind of stuck between things. Like maybe I'll be doing carpentry. But after that, I might want to go to college to learn more. Maybe engineering—that would be good for me since I know math. Maybe that plus carpentry will get me a good job. I've heard that Purdue has a good engineering department—maybe we'll go there and live in the student housing they have for married couples with kids.

"At thirty, I could be a guy who works sometimes in an office somewhere, doing paperwork, and then other days in my work clothes building stuff. That's what my math teacher told me—you can have more fun designing buildings and *then* working on them, if I want to. That way, I could work on bridges, or roads, or almost anything that needs designing."

Jamie pauses, remembering something else. "I also like laying carpet. My cousin does that and he earns lots of money, sometimes $2,000 in two weeks. It's hard work, though—you got to measure right, and you got to be real strong to lift the rolls of carpet. But when you're done, it looks really nice, and you'd feel

In the future, Jamie contemplates attending either a trade school to learn carpentry or pursuing a degree in engineering. In the meantime, however, he works part-time at a discount store to help support his family.

good, knowing that someone's going to be living there walking around on that carpet. I'd like to make a lot of money doing that while I'm still in high school—maybe in the summer or something. That would be good to save for college."

"I WANT HER TO BE GLAD SHE WAS BORN"

There are many things he wants for his daughter, he says, but her happiness is most important.

"I hope she'll be great at something," he smiles. "It would be fun to see her getting real good at school, or sports, or music or something. But the happiness part is way more important. I want her to be glad she was born, mostly. So even if times are hard, or money is tight in our family, there is still happiness. We love each other, and that will make her feel glad.

"I know something else, and that's that I'm going to be one strict father! I mean, I'll let her do things within reason, things she wants to do. But she can't stay out all night, and she can't be bringing her boyfriends around here when she's young. I'll stick to those rules, I know.

"I'll send her to an all-girls school, too. No public schools, where they have gangs everywhere you look. I'm not afraid of them myself, but they got no business in the same school with my daughter. And if she was doing some drugs, I'd be real sad. I'd spank her, find out who gave them to her, and then I'd call the cops and have them arrest the guy. I wouldn't fool around, no. Stuff like that's just too important to just let slide."

James stops to catch his breath, and continues.

"I don't want her coming up pregnant at no young age, that's all. It worked out okay so far for me and Elishai, but it's hard. I mean, we're young and all that, and we don't have much. We don't even live together, so it's like I got to keep remembering we're a family. But it don't seem like it sometimes when I'm home at my mama's house, and she's home at her house.

"I worry sometimes that it won't last," he admits, scowling a little. "I think about how it would be if something went wrong, and me and Elishai wouldn't stay together. Then I think, what if something goes wrong, what will happen with the baby? We both love our daughter, I know that. And sometimes when I hear about people staying together for the sake of their kids, I understand why they would do that. I don't want nothing to go wrong, that's the main thing. Anyway, that's why I don't want my daughter to start as early as me in being a parent."

"We Usually Don't Have Big Huge Fights"

Asked if there is any concrete reason why he worries about breaking up with Elishai, Jamie shakes his head.

"No reason," he says. "I don't think we will, because we usually don't have big huge fights. We never had a fistfight or nothing like that. Lots of people I know do that, but I don't like it. It's not right to be laying your hands that way on your wife or your girlfriend. Me and Elishai stop before either one of us gets real mad.

"The thing about both me and Elishai is that we don't want our daughter growing up in that kind of home, where people are violent and she hears a lot of bad language and stuff. Then before you know it, she's talking like that, too, and then we're wondering how come she's got that trash coming out of her mouth. But then, see, we'd have to blame ourselves, because it was us that taught her, just by our example.

"Same with fighting," he continues. "If she sees us hitting and being physical with our problems, that teaches her that she can do that, too. If I feel like me and Elishai are getting close to those feelings, where it might turn out that we say or do things we can't take back, I just go home. By the time I get all the way back over here, I'll call her from my mama's house. By then, we are both cooled off and can talk it over. That's best."

"It's the Most Important Thing I Ever Done"

Jamie runs his hands down his face, deep in thought. He stops before a banged-up locker and opens it quickly.

"One thing is you know when you have a kid what is most important. Like I never really used to worry about too many things. Once, when my brother was shot, I worried. I was really *scared*. I even wrote a song for my brother, a rap song, and made a tape of it. It was kind of a release or something. I thought it was really good.

"I played it for my brother after he got better, after he was out of the hospital. He heard it and told me not to send it in to no record company, because it was too personal. I think he liked that I did it, but he didn't think it was right to share it. Maybe it reminded him too much of getting shot, I don't know.

"But anyway, aside from that, I never really worried that much about other people, unless it had something to do with me. Man! That changed with Easha being born! I worry about her getting sick, or her getting hurt now that she's learning how to walk. I think about her riding her bike someday on the road; I think about her falling down in some playground. I even thought about her getting her feelings hurt by some teacher in school, like if she was trying hard and some stupid teacher makes fun of her for making a mistake. It's not good to go looking for trouble, I know that. But when I think about stuff like that, it makes me get real knotted up inside, like I want to protect her. Protecting her—it's the most important thing I ever done."

ONE SCARY TIME

Jamie remembers that his fears for Easha were grounded in something real only once, when the baby became sick while she was at his house for the weekend.

"That was the most scary time," he says, sighing. "I knew she was sick, but I wasn't sure what to do. She was real hot. I was feeling her head and she was just burning up. I said to my mama, 'She's really sick—we got to do something!'

"We took her temperature and it was 101 degrees, which is pretty high. We rushed her to the hospital, and they kept her there overnight. The next day she started getting better. But the doctor told us that it was a reaction, that's why she got sick. It was because people were smoking around her, and she can't be around no smoke like that.

"It isn't Elishai that smokes, it's me. It's my worst habit," he says, irritated with himself. "I was smoking in the room with her and she got sick. I felt real bad, but I learned that that baby can't be around *any* smoke. I keep all the smokers away from her. And if I want a cigarette, I go outside, even if it's raining or it's real cold. Then I come inside, go into the bathroom and brush my teeth, so I don't smell like smoke. I don't ever want her getting sick like that again."

"SHE'S STRONG AND TOUGH"

Otherwise, Jamie says that his daughter has been very healthy.

"She's strong and tough, too," he says proudly. "She's always trying to walk, trying to hold on to things and scoot around. She falls all the time—she can't help it. That's what learning to walk is

(From left to right) Jamie poses with his girlfriend, Elishai; his sister; and his mother. Jamie admits, "It worked out okay so far for me and Elishai, but it's hard. I mean, we're young and all that, and we don't have much."

all about, my mama says. But Easha usually doesn't cry. She just picks herself back up and keeps doing whatever she was doing. She walks around getting her dolls or her animals, whatever. She likes to carry things now in her one hand while she's walking, that's her new thing. Even if it's just a little piece of paper, she'll be holding on to it. Maybe it's for balance or something, I don't know. She has fun, though.

"She loves to swing, loves to play in that sandbox, loves to be outside. She's getting to talk a little now, too. She says 'Daddy,' 'Mama,' 'eat-eat'—stuff like that. One day I came into the house, and she's like, 'Daddy' plain as day. I said, 'Oh my God! She said my name!' It was a real good feeling.

"And she loves kissing, hugging. I can't say no to her, she's so cute. She gets everybody hugging and kissing, too. My little cousin, he don't like it much. He's like three or something. Easha's always kissing him on the cheek, following him around. We was teasing him about that, too!"

"WHAT CAN I DO?"

For now, Jamie says, he's going to work hard and spend as much time as he can with his daughter. Homework and his jobs get in the way, but he's determined.

"I'll show you proof of how my dedication is," he laughs, pointing to his longish hair. "Look at this hair! I need it cut, real bad. I mean, I know it looks stupid. But I'm going to let it grow more, so I don't have to get so many haircuts. My hair gets real long, and then I'll cut it. For sure I'll cut it this summer, because it gets real hot when it's long.

"But I'm doing that for my daughter, too, just like I got this stupid-looking pair of shoes and stuff. I'd rather spend the money on her. It's a lot more fun for me to see her looking good. Hey, what can I do?" he shrugs with a smile. "I'm her father—that's what fathers are supposed to be doing!"

Brad

"I WAS EXCITED ABOUT THE KID,
YEAH. BUT I WASN'T EXCITED
ABOUT THE RESPONSIBILITY."

*Author's Note: I met Brad through a counselor in a young father's pro-
gram. The counselor mentioned that Brad and his girlfriend had issues to
work out before any sort of family situation could be created for them and
their new daughter.*

*He's a nice boy—like Jamie, soft-spoken and a little shy at first. His
youth is most apparent when he talks about how embarrassed he was to
purchase condoms after he and his girlfriend became sexually active. In
fact, he admits, the only condoms he used were grabbed by a friend at a
clinic. After they ran out, says Brad, he didn't buy more. I am tempted to
roll my eyes when this father mentions being nervous about being seen
buying condoms, and I think to myself, How high school!, when I realize
that that's just what Brad is—a high school kid.*

*The lack of parental involvement and supervision contributed mightily
to the conception of a child: Brad was always alone at home in the
evenings, and his girlfriend's parents evidently did not realize that their
daughter had been sexually active since age eleven and took no steps to
control her activities.*

It is a rainy, cold March afternoon in this remote suburb, and the
stair carpeting in the small apartment building is muddy and wet.
A school bus has just let out a handful of children near the building, and two of them clamber to get into the entryway out of the
rain.

On the second floor Brad opens the door to the apartment he
shares with his mother. He is a big kid, seventeen but with

something of a baby face. His hair is very short, and he covers most of it with a Green Bay Packers stocking cap. He wears over-sized blue jeans with a thick silver chain leading from belt loop to pocket. Brad turns the television volume down, and motions for his visitors to have a seat.

His mother waves and calls hello to the visitors from the kitchen. She sits quietly at the kitchen table, smoking a cigarette and listening to her son talk.

Although seventeen-year-old Brad is a father, he seldom sees his daughter, Jordan. "I'm not even talking to my kid's mother now," he explains. "She told me not to bother calling, because she and the baby both hate me."

"The Best Word Would Be 'Stressful'"

Brad is clearly not yet in the "fatherhood mode." Belated congratulations on the birth of this teenager's new baby are met with a sort of hopeless, confused shrug.

"I don't know how to react," he says frankly in a surprisingly soft voice. "I'm not even talking to my kid's mother now. Last time I talked to her, she told me not to bother calling, because she and the baby both hate me.

"If I had to pick a word to categorize my emotions about Jordan being born, I guess it wouldn't be something like 'happy' or 'sad' or something like that. The best word would be 'stressful.' Before she was born, before all this happened, my life was just being normal, I guess. I was just being a teenager, turning sixteen and getting ready to look for a job, hanging with my friends.

"But now I have stuff I'm supposed to be doing. Kim—Jordan's mother—she has it all mapped out for me. And it's like weird, because we're parents together, and we had broken up long before Jordan was born. And I get some pressure from my mom and my older sister, too. I just feel like I'm being pulled a lot of different directions at once. Right now, I don't feel like going any direction at all."

"I Just Went Up and Introduced Myself"

It's impossible to understand his feelings about the birth of his daughter, he agrees, without understanding his relationship with Kim, his previous girlfriend, the mother of his child.

"She was fourteen when all this happened," he says. "I was two years older. I'd met her at the bus stop; she lived in the apartment right across the road, and I didn't even know it. She doesn't live there now, but then she did. Kim was sort of new around here. I just saw her the first day of school. I just went up and introduced myself."

Brad admits that this was not typical behavior for him. "I was usually kind of shy, kind of quiet," he shrugs. "I hadn't had any real serious girlfriends before, so I guess I was kind of surprised myself that I'd made the first move. But she seemed kind of lost, and kind of looking for a friend, so I talked to her. She said her name was Kim, and that she was from North Carolina. She was easy to talk to, acted real friendly.

"Anyway, she was really pretty—blond and thin. She said she was starting eighth grade at the same area learning center I went

Brad's mother looks on as her son discusses what it is like to be a teen father. "I'm real open with my mom," Brad says. "I can talk to her about anything."

to, but I was starting my sophomore year. We obviously weren't going to be in any classes together, but we saw each other around—in the halls, in the commons, stuff like that."

GETTING ALONG

Brad and Kim began seeing each other after school, which soon led to a more serious relationship.

"One time I just invited her to my apartment after school. She brought a couple of her friends, and I invited a couple of mine. That first time, we just hung out, watching television and stuff. I remember she wasn't as talkative then as she was when it was just us two talking, like at the bus stop. But it was pretty nice, even when her friends were around.

"We kind of started hanging around a lot after school. Sometimes me and my friends would play basketball—see, I have a hoop outside. And Kim and some of her friends would walk over and sit on the grass and watch us play. During the summer it was almost every day. Just real low-key, you know, nothing much. But it was fun having her around."

Brad says that he got along fairly well with Kim's parents, too.

"Her dad was especially nice," he says. "He'd crack jokes and talk to me about different things. Her mom, though, I was never really sure about. She was kind of hard to read. She had this look she'd give me sometimes, like she really didn't like me, but I'm not sure if that was really it. I don't know—I never felt really comfortable around her. But even so, they weren't against us going out, even though there was a difference in our ages. And they never said, you know, 'You two are seeing too much of each other,' like some parents might."

When did their relationship become sexual? As he is about to answer, a telephone rings, and his mother, still seated nearby at the kitchen table, answers it quietly. Asked if he is uncomfortable talking about these matters with his mother present, Brad shakes his head quickly.

"No, not at all," he says. "I'm real open with my mom—I can talk to her about anything. Anyway, as far as the sexual part, I'm pretty sure it was about four months from when we first met—I'm not exactly positive. I *do* remember being surprised that Kim wanted to do it right away, I mean, immediately. I wanted to wait a little bit, I guess. It was my first time, but not hers. She told me she'd lost her virginity at eleven; I asked her about that, but she never wanted to talk about it."

"SHE THREW THEM OUT THE WINDOW"

Brad stresses that he did ask Kim about protection, and she assured him that she was on the pill. However, he soon learned that Kim was less than careful to take it regularly.

"When we started having sex, she told me she was on the pill, because yeah, I was worried about her getting pregnant," he says. "So I didn't worry about anything then. But one day I was looking at her pouch where she carried her stuff, and the little package of pills had some days that still hadn't been taken—and these were days that had already gone by. So I asked her why she hadn't taken them.

"All she did was get mad," he says with contempt. "And then she just took the little plastic container the pills were in and she threw them out the window! Really! I asked her, 'What did you do that for?' and she said she wanted kids—that she liked kids. So then I started realizing that I had to be the one to use protection."

Brad went to his friend Mike, who was nineteen. He explained what had happened with Kim's pills, and asked Mike what he thought was the best thing to do.

"He's older, you know, so I thought he'd give me good advice," says Brad honestly. "He told me that I should take responsibility and use condoms if I still wanted to keep having sex with her. I did—so I did."

"I KIND OF FELT REAL DUMB ABOUT DOING THAT"

Mike even offered to help out by going to the doctor's office and getting free condoms for Brad.

"He grabbed a whole handful for me," he says. "And that was great, for a while. But then, when the supply ran out, I stopped using them. See, it was real uncomfortable for me to just go out and buy them myself, like in a drugstore or whatever. If I went to the Festival or another store around here, everyone would know what I was doing. It's a pretty small town, and that would be embarrassing. I kind of felt real dumb doing that."

So, he admits, they stopped using any protection at all, a fact that makes him feel foolish now.

"I think about that now, about how easy it would have been to get someone to buy them for me or whatever, and I want to kick myself. But back a year ago, it just felt too weird. But the result is that I'm a father, with a girlfriend who hates my guts.

"There's no question in my mind, looking back, that she wanted to get pregnant. I have no idea why. But she kept saying she liked kids. And I was busy being a coward about getting condoms. So I guess the breakdown occurred on both sides. It wasn't just her fault any more than mine."

THE FRIENDS

Besides understanding his relationship with Kim, Brad insists, it's important to understand the cause of the vast majority of their quarrels—his friends.

"I've had these friends forever," he says with conviction. "They've always been there for me—I spend more time with them than anyone. And when I started having a sexual relationship with Kim, I spent no time with them anymore. Everything changed a lot. I was spending like every minute with her—all my time. So I basically lost those friends for a real long time.

After Brad (center) started having a sexual relationship with Kim, he quit spending time with his friends. "It made me feel bad," he recalls, "because those friends have been my life, since I was pretty young."

"They knew why I wasn't around, yeah. I mean, I never really talked to them about it—except Mike—but they just figured it out, I guess. They'd say, 'Oh, Brad's home doing his thing.' But it made me feel bad, because those friends have been my life, since I was pretty young. But it was just me and Kim, then, hanging around at my house, having sex there. My mom was at work, so we had the place to ourselves."

Brad says that although he and Kim usually got along, she never really liked his friends, and that was always a sore spot between them.

"She called them a bunch of losers, a bunch of drug addicts who get me into trouble," he complains. "I don't see it like she does, not at all. I know they do smoke a little—so do I on occasion. And they like to party, but there's nothing wrong with that that I know. I mean, drinking a little bit isn't so bad."

FIVE DAYS OF DOING TIME

Brad admits, however, that he *has* gotten into trouble with his older friends, but is adamant that it happened almost four years ago and that it was his own fault as much as theirs.

"I was thirteen," he says. "We made a couple of bombs. It was no big deal, really. We had seen it on the news—they explained how to do it right on TV. We didn't blow anything up, just set them off in the sand. But it bothered the neighbors, and the fact that the things were bombs made it worse.

"I got locked away for five days; it doesn't sound like much, but it was the longest five days of my life. I got yelled at constantly when I was there. I was one of the youngest guys there, and it was really scary. Just on the other side of our building were the long-term sex offenders. My mom would come up there and see me for a little while, and I remember watching her walk away. I was really sad; I'd cry.

"So anyway, that took place way before I met Kim, but she acts like my friends are just waiting for a chance to get me in trouble. They don't, though. They're just older, got more time on their hands. Most have already graduated or dropped out. They don't have girlfriends or anything; most of them live with their parents. So we spend the days shooting hoops, playing hackysack, watching TV, or whatever."

"I Just Wait Until They're Ready to Go"

The one thing about his friends that makes Kim angriest, he says, is that because he spends so much time with them, he often skips school.

"I won't argue that I haven't let school slide," he admits. "It's tough to go. It's hard for me to get up early every day—it's as simple as that. I'm not bad in school; I do good work when I'm there, maybe two or three days a week. I did get in a little trouble for a while, because of that. The problem is that I'm just too tired to go. I'd sleep, then yeah, I wake up and I *could* go, but it's only a couple hours, and then I think, why bother?"

Asked why he is so tired every morning, Brad looks a little uncomfortable.

"No, it's not work," he says. "I don't have a job. My friends come over here almost every night; they stay until real late. That kind of keeps me from going to bed. And no, I can't just tell them to go home. I don't like to be mean—I can't do that. I just wait until they're ready to go, and I lock up and go to bed. It's usually midnight or 1:00 A.M. before they leave, or later on the weekends.

"My mom—she doesn't really mind," he continues. "See, she works during the week at a factory, making circuit boards. She works from six in the evening till six in the morning, so she's not here. Anyway, that's the deal that's an issue between me and Kim—my friends and their 'bad influence' on me."

HEARING THE NEWS

After several months Kim's period was late, and she mentioned it to Brad at school one morning.

"I was kind of worried," he says. "At my school, there's a day care for some of the students who have kids—let them stay there while the moms are taking classes. And there's a teen mom adviser—I went to talk to her. She went and talked to Kim, and they left together to go to the Planned Parenthood office, where Kim could get a pregnancy test."

Brad grins a little, knowing how strange it sounds that he could walk right up to a teen mom adviser at his school, when months before he was too embarrassed to buy condoms at the store.

"I know," he says. "It's weird. But, I don't know, at my school, I pretty much know everybody. I know all the teachers, and I don't feel dumb talking to them, I guess. It didn't make me uncomfortable, maybe just because what was most important was finding out about Kim being pregnant. I think one positive thing that's happened out of this whole deal is that I've gotten more open about things. That's a change—it's not the way I've ever been. Now I'll say if something is important to me. I'll say what I want, and if I don't understand, I'll ask the question.

"Anyway—the pregnancy test. So the first time I saw Kim later that day, she walked right by without saying anything to me. I ran after her and when I caught up with her, I just said, 'So?' And she said, 'Well, I'm pregnant.' Just like that. And then she just turned and walked away. She looked real sad. I don't remember too much about it—I think I was too shocked. I just stood there and watched her leave."

CONFRONTATION

Brad remembers that he knew he needed to spend some time alone, just to think.

"I went to the commons area, and I just sat at a table by myself. I was really scared, just thinking about the words she said, how she

Brad says he was overwhelmed by the news of his girlfriend's pregnancy. After informing their parents, Brad says, "First thing I did was go out and look for a whole bunch of jobs."

looked. I wondered, Could that test be wrong? and, What if we go and tell our parents, and they get angry, and then we find out that it was a false alarm—what then? I know I was just being afraid to face up to the whole thing. I hadn't even faced up to Kim yet.

"So later the same day, I told my mom. I went inside and she was doing dishes. I said, 'Kim's pregnant.' She just turned around and said, 'Now what are you going to do?' Just like that. I told her that I was going to get a job, get everything together, and try to be ready when the kid was born. My mom just looked at me and said, 'It's your problem now, so you've got to deal with it.' I was surprised that she wasn't mad at me, or yell or something."

It was far more difficult to tell her parents the news, says Brad.

"I had told Kim that I would try to be big about it and tell them myself," he says. "I said I should be the one. So after dinner I called over there, and told Kim's mom that I had to tell them something, that I'd be right over.

"Well, I told them right away, right when I got there. Her mom and dad were just sitting on the sofa, watching television. The first thing they did was to send Kim to her room. They told me to come over and sit with them, because they wanted to talk to me. Man, that was so hard. It was just me, and I had to sit right in between them, her mom on one side and her dad on the other. They were mad, yeah. Even her dad, who had always been the nicer one. And I didn't do much talking; they were doing all of it, and asking me lots of questions.

"It was real bad," he says. "They were just talking one and then the other, back and forth across me. They asked me how I was going to get a job, how would I be able to support myself, let alone a kid. They said that if things got tough, they weren't going to want to have Kim and the kid live there, so what was I going to do? I told them, 'I'll just find some way that I can do all of this.' They kept saying over and over, 'We're not going to help you, we're not going to help you.'"

"Too Far Away"

There was some relief just in telling his mother and Kim's parents, Brad agrees, but it was very short-lived.

"It was good that the telling was over, but I had so much to think about, so much to do," he says. "First thing I did was go out and look for a whole bunch of jobs. I brought home a whole stack of applications from everywhere around here. I filled them all out, returned them, and waited.

"Only one place called me back. It was a manager at Burger King, over here on the highway. I worked there for a while as just a guy, you know, a guy behind the counter. But I quit that after a little bit—a lot of people didn't like me, I think. One of the other workers threw something in my face—I didn't even know her! I left that day, and never went back. So ever since then, I've been looking for another job. I'm not working even now, no. I'm not making any money at all."

To make things even more stressful, Brad says, his relationship with Kim began to sour.

"It's not that she was mad at me, or I was mad at her," he explains. "It's just that what we did was so different. Our conversations sure changed a lot. It was stuff like talking about names, about what it was going to be like after the kid was born, stuff like that. We decided that I would get to choose the baby's first name, and Kim would choose the middle name.

"I wanted Michael if it was a boy, and Jordan for a girl. I came up with that once when I was talking to one of my friends. I'm a Bulls fan, you can tell. But Kim liked the idea okay, like I said, just as long as she got to pick the middle name.

"But it still didn't feel the same when we went out. It just didn't feel like going out. She was tired a lot, and she didn't feel as much like having sex. And after a while, talking about the kid didn't even seem real. She was like two or three months along, and it seemed too far away. I was excited about the kid, yeah. But I wasn't excited about the responsibility. I felt two different ways."

SPLITTING UP

After a few months, Brad began to feel as though he and Kim were drifting apart.

"We couldn't get together; it didn't seem like she wanted to," he shrugs. "She was hanging around with her friends, and not even calling me. I'd be paging her all day, but she'd never call me back. And then somebody told me that they'd seen her out somewhere, and she had been cheating on me. That made me so mad!

"Anyway, I called her one morning, and we argued about it. I don't know—it was just a big fight for a while. We kind of got back together for a little while, because she told me she really cared about me. But it's hard to explain—it just wasn't the same anymore.

"The same thing happened again, not long after we'd gotten back together. People were telling me stories about her cheating on me. I got mad at her, and she just got all defensive. It was stupid; it just seemed like we couldn't solve anything without yelling at each other. When I confronted her about the cheating, she got really angry. She'd say, 'Yeah, right—I'm pregnant and I'm cheating on you.' Like that, really sarcastic.

"So I just broke it off. I said, 'Well, it's over for now. I'll still take care of you, and I'll call you and talk to you. I'll take care of my responsibilities, but as far as us, we're done now.' She just said that was okay, because she knew I'd come back after a while. She'd call every once in a while, but that was about all the contact we had."

Brad says that he didn't like her calls because she tried to give him orders and ultimatums.

A devoted basketball fan, Brad named his daughter Jordan after NBA star Michael Jordan.

"She was basically being my mom," he says, "and I didn't like it. She'd tell me my friends were spending way too much time over here, and that they should start leaving by 10:00 every night so I could do homework and get to bed. She said I had to start taking responsibility, getting myself up for school every day. I got mad and yelled at her to stop being my mother. So, I guess we just stopped talking completely."

"I Stayed Away"

Not only weren't Brad and Kim talking, they never saw each other. Kim's parents had transferred her to another school because they felt she wasn't learning as much where she and Brad had been.

"I'm not saying this to be mean, but she's not real bright," he explains. "She gets really bad grades. The switch didn't have anything to do with her being pregnant, I don't think. So I didn't ever see her during the day, and we weren't talking on the phone.

"She was due to have the baby sometime before Christmas, but she was overdue. The doctors were going to induce her, hook her up to some medicine that would start her labor. Anyway, my friends and I left on Christmas night. None of us knew she was going to be induced the next day, but she was. We just were having a party, going around to people's houses, having fun.

"But I came back the next day, and my sister and my mom had gone to the hospital; my mom had talked to Kim's mom and had found out that she was going to have the kid any minute. So they took off for the hospital."

His place might have been with Kim, Brad concedes, but he had no interest in being there for the birth of his child.

"I didn't want to go down there; I worried that I'd get looked at weird," he admits. "I hadn't talked to her, hadn't even known she was going to have the baby on December 26. I was excited, yeah, and pretty curious. But I stayed away."

"She Was Really Beautiful"

It would have been impossible for him to stay away for long, he admits reluctantly. Curiosity about the new baby (his mother and sister had told him it was a girl) made him eager for more details.

"I kept wondering about what she looked like, if she looked anything like me," he says. "I knew from my mom that she weighed in at 8 pounds, 4 ounces when she was born, and that's pretty good sized. I knew she had blond hair, too. I was real interested—I admit that—but I couldn't figure out a way to see the baby without getting into a scene with her or her parents. I was afraid, yeah.

"I didn't go to the hospital at all, but when she came home with the baby, she had her mom drop her and the baby over at my house. Did I say her name is Jordan Lee? Lee, that's the middle

Pictures of Brad's daughter, Jordan, are scattered across the coffee table. Brad's quarrelsome relationship with Kim, coupled with his fear of being a parent, kept him away from the hospital when Jordan was born.

name that Kim picked out. I just sat in the chair—this one where I'm sitting in now. My mom and Kim and my sister were all talking and oohing and ahhing over her, but I wasn't saying anything. I was too scared to hold the baby. I was too scared to talk to Kim. So I just sat on the chair, watching everybody else hold the baby.

"But then my mom must have understood how I was feeling or something, because she just came over and put the baby in my arms. I didn't even have time to think about it. And I just sat there with her for about twenty minutes, just looking at her. She was really beautiful, just sleeping. And once I held her, I felt more comfortable about talking to Kim."

Brad says that for a moment it seemed that they might be able to get back together.

"It was really nice, just sitting holding my baby, looking at Kim. She looked happy; I felt proud. But then, it just seemed like things went bad. She started talking about all the things I had to start doing, all the changes I had to make. Same stuff as before—lose my friends, go to school, get a job. It was too much for me; we haven't talked about getting back together since then. And I haven't even seen or talked to her in almost four weeks. It doesn't seem like there is a two-parent family in Jordan's future."

"HE NEVER EVEN CALLED"

The last statement is painful for Brad to make, and he goes quiet, as though he is thinking of the enormity of Jordan Lee's problem.

"I wouldn't wish that on anyone," he says. "My mom and dad have been divorced for eleven years now. I haven't seen him in four years. And I don't want my kid to go through the same thing I did when I was growing up. I missed having a dad, someone to show me different things. I mean, I can't even think of a specific thing—just everything. Someone to ask about things, someone to have around, just to do things with. My mom always worked, so it was just me and my sister. And she's moved out now, so it's just the two of us here, me and my mom.

"I don't think my dad and I were ever close, even before they split up. When they were first separated, my dad would stop by once in a while. He'd always act like we were going to do fun stuff together; he'd always talk about it. But then he never followed through. We never did anything. So, no, I guess we weren't close. I wanted to be, but I guess he didn't. Or maybe he couldn't, or something.

"And so now, we don't have any contact at all. It's kind of weird. Last winter, about two days before Jordan was born, I went over to where my dad lives now. I hadn't seen him in a really long time. I was going to tell him about the fact that I was going to have a kid soon. I don't even know why I thought about telling him, when I wasn't even talking much about it with my friends.

"But anyway, I went over there, and his girlfriend was there. He was out somewhere. I told her about the whole thing, about Kim and the baby that was going to be born soon, and she told me she'd tell him when he came home. But that was four months ago, and I never heard from him. He never even called."

TRYING TO STAY INVOLVED

Even though he and Kim weren't on the best of terms, counselors urged him not to let that stand in the way of his getting to know his baby. He was assigned a parenting class—with Kim and Jordan—every Wednesday during school time.

"Those weren't bad classes," he says. "You learn a lot of stuff about how to take care of the baby, nutrition, the kind of medical care babies need. It was all pretty interesting. Kim and I talked a little, yeah, but it wasn't about anything other than Jordan, and how to take care of her. Like, she gets lots of gas from the formula she was on, stuff like that.

"My counselor was glad I was doing these classes; he was really trying to urge me not to get depressed about things. He told me to look after my rights as a father, to get a job, to get as involved with Jordan's life as I can. I know he understands that it's hard for me to get *too* involved, since Kim and I don't get along. But I've done some stuff—I've bought some clothes and stuff for Jordan, just some small stuff. I don't have any money to speak of, but I'm not going to be poor forever."

Although Brad is as anxious as Kim that he get a job, he refuses to budge on the issue of his friends.

"I couldn't ever give them up, no," he says in an offended tone. "Not totally. I mean, my friends were here long before Jordan; I wouldn't give them up. They'll always be here, they'll always be with me. I'm not saying that they have to be here every minute, like they are now—I know they're here from 2:30 when I get home from school until midnight or so. But if Jordan were here more often, they wouldn't be around when she was here. I wouldn't mind that, no. It would work out."

"MY MOM FELT REAL BAD"

Brad says that quarreling with Kim has had far-reaching effects—effects he would not have anticipated.

"You know before, when I said that Kim got mad a few weeks ago? Well, that's the time we had that big fight, where she said I wasn't a good parent, because I'm not even a part-time parent. She says that whenever she wants to go out and asks me to spend some time watching Jordan, I never will. But that's not fair. She never asks me. She just *assumes* that I wouldn't, because she knew my friends would probably be here.

"So she gets all furious, and says some mean things, like about how she and Jordan hate me a lot. And I know deep down she doesn't mean that Jordan hates me—I mean, how can a baby hate anyone? But she's mad because she thinks I'm choosing my friends over her. I know in my head that's what she's really angry about, but in my heart, it hurts a lot. And I sometimes think about her telling Jordan about me when she's older, how she'll say, 'Your father's a bad person; it isn't worth you getting to know him.' I mean, that could happen—you hear about kids being told that by their mother.

"So the last thing that happened, is after that fight, my mom felt real bad. She was worried that whatever happens between Kim and me will affect whether she gets to see Jordan. And Jordan's her granddaughter, so yeah, she has a real interest in how it works out. So she calls Kim's mom the next day, and tells her that she wants to make sure that she can still be a grandma to Jordan, that she'll get to see her.

"But then Kim went crazy. She called me all kinds of names, and she said, 'What's all this B.S. about your mom getting a lawyer and getting visitation rights, and all that?' She said, 'I don't need this!' She told me that my mom can see Jordan whenever she wants, but not me, because she hates me.

"So for now, I'm not allowed to have Jordan over here, not unless Kim is here, too. But Kim won't come because of my friends. It just goes around and around, same thing, same thing. I told her that if she and Jordan came, I'd make sure my friends aren't here,

76

Brad would like to be a typical seventeen-year-old, but he is burdened by the demands of fatherhood, including the overwhelming need to financially support his daughter.

that it would just be us. But she doesn't believe me—she just says, 'Yeah, right, it won't happen.' So what do you do?"

LOOKING FOR A PLAN

Right now, Brad feels as though he is in a room with lots of doors that all seem to be locked.

"It's like, where do I start?" he says. "Next year I'm going to be a senior, she'll just be starting tenth grade. If we got along, then what? I mean, if we hadn't had all these fights, if we were really tight, would things be a lot different? Would we get married? Would we go live somewhere and me get a job? Would that work with her being fifteen?

"The reality is, if I work real hard and try to make up those classes I didn't pass when I wasn't going to school, I'll graduate. But then what? I used to think about being a pediatrician or something like that, back a long time ago. Something that would be fun, and you'd make a lot of money. And Kim—she never talked about anything, no goals or anything. She didn't have plans like some people had. I don't know of any interests she had, looking back on when we were together. She was interested in me. But I don't know what else.

"So what do I do? I can't afford college, and my grades aren't that good, anyway. I've thought about the military, maybe the air force or the navy. My cousin's in the navy now, and he's told me a lot of stuff about that. So that's a possibility.

"But then, I'm not supporting Jordan at all. I feel so bad about that, because I promised Kim, and her parents, and my mom that I would. And myself—I promised myself. I'd be willing to quit school right now and go after a real job, but my mom won't let me. I know she's smart, but I feel stressed out that time's going by, and there's no support from me. Money's really scarce. I don't even drive yet!"

THE BAD GUY

Brad is as confused about his relationship with Kim as he is toward his daughter.

"I don't even know if I want to get back with her," he admits. "I'm seeing a girl now—an old friend of Kim's. And needless to say, she's not interested in getting into a serious relationship with me. I know one thing—I won't be having any more kids. That will never happen. Protection for me, protection for the girl, absolutely. This time, I know I can stick to that. The last thing I'll worry about is being embarrassed buying condoms.

"But if I did want to get back with Kim, I don't even know if she'd want me. She's got another boyfriend, too, and he's a guy I used to be friends with! I'm not sure how serious they are. I know her mom watches Jordan a lot when Kim goes out. Her parents sure aren't holding to their threat of not helping out with the baby."

If you ask his mother or sister, Brad says, he is confident that they'll tell you he is the bad guy in all of this.

"I know my mom is loyal to me," he begins, "but she doesn't like what's happening. She and my sister start going on about how Jordan is the cutest baby, she's the smartest baby, stuff like that, and I know they're both blaming me. I'm letting everybody down—Kim, her parents, Jordan, my mom, my sister—you name it. Everybody loves Jordan, and if it weren't for me—."

He shakes his head and rubs his hands over his face.

"I don't disagree with them. I'm probably being a bad guy. But I can't do it any other way right now. Not right now, with Kim being so mad. I really don't know how else to do it. I haven't talked to my friends much about Kim, and they never bring her up, or Jordan either. One of my friends did ask me last Friday about her, and I said I didn't really know anything. It was kind of coincidence, because I'd been thinking about calling her that day. He said to me, 'You know, Brad, if you want to go over there, we'll go over there—I'll take you.' But I thought about it for a while, and I said no. I just got scared."

William

"I DON'T WANT TO WISH HIM AWAY, BUT . . . I WISH WE COULD HAVE WAITED TO HAVE A BABY."

Author's Note: William is a nineteen-year-old teen whose future as a father seems tied up with his future as a law-abiding citizen. His past is a source of shame to him, especially when he thinks about sliding back into his former life of drug dealing and robbery, and the effect of his criminal activities on his ability to raise his son. If, as he claims, he is done with that life, he seems capable of becoming a very caring father, for little Damon is clearly the most precious thing in his life.

For now, he worries. His lack of a job—or any real optimism for the future—makes him edgy and nervous, as does his fear that his former drug-dealing competitors may find out where he is living and hurt his family. He worries, too, that his relationship with his girlfriend (now pregnant with their second child) might not last. He admits he uses marijuana and alcohol to counteract his nervousness, knowing that these substances are dangerous for him (he has battled drug and alcohol abuse since he was very young). William is likable and open, and I find myself pulling for him to succeed.

A Native American teenager looks through the curtain in the living room, unwilling to answer the doorbell right away. When he realizes his suspicions are unfounded, he opens the door, smiling a bit self-consciously.

"I didn't know when you were coming," he says in a loud voice. "I never like it when the doorbell rings unless I'm sure who's out there."

William is just nineteen, slightly overweight, with a scraggly beard sprouting on his chin. He is wearing dark pants and a white T-shirt. From inside the house comes the sound of a baby crying.

"Come on in," he says smiling. "Nap time is over, I think."

GROWING UP LAKOTA

"I'm a Lakota Sioux," he explains, making himself comfortable on the sofa. "From South Dakota. Not like the Dakota Sioux from

Nineteen-year-old William is the father of a fifteen-month-old son, Damon, and his girlfriend is currently pregnant with their second child. "I've lived a lot in nineteen years," William confides. "There's a lot more to me than just being a father."

Minnesota. I grew up back in Rapid City, came here in 1991. I didn't live on a reservation, no. Just lived in the town."

William stops a moment, listening to a conversation in the kitchen. He shakes his head quickly and smiles.

"I thought someone out there was calling me. This is my mom's house, not mine. Me and Cathy—that's my girlfriend—and little Damon are just staying here for a little while, until we get a place. We'll be gone real soon, probably within the week.

"Anyway, where was I? Oh, right, Rapid City. I didn't have no spectacular childhood—just average, I guess. School was okay for a while, but then—you know."

He beams with a wicked smile. "You know how it gets, after a while. One day you like it, and then you don't. I was an all-right student. I actually did a little better when I was in jail, I think."

William knows this last sentence has piqued the interest of his visitors, and he beams again. "I've lived a lot in nineteen years, you know. There's a lot more to me than just being a father, I'll tell you that!"

He holds out his right hand, displaying three round scars on its back.

"See there?" he asks. "Cigarette burns. That's what me and my friends used to do in Rapid City. Make cigarette burns on our hands, being big men." He grins, shaking his head. "Stupid stuff."

FAMILY LIFE

William maintains that although some social workers might have labeled his family dysfunctional, it never really seemed abnormal to him.

"My mom had me when she was fourteen years old," he says. "Dad wasn't around at all—I don't know a whole lot about him. My uncle was around, though. He was kind of the man figure in our house. My mom was gone a lot, so she wasn't the mom figure—she was just a kid, going all over the place. So my grandma was the mom; she did a real good job, I think.

"I have a younger brother, Jason. He's seventeen now. And I got a sister, Patricia, and a little brother who's eleven now. But my grandma was in charge. I don't remember spending time feeling sorry for myself that my mom wasn't around for me. I learned to get along with my grandma, and that was great. We were real close.

"Sometimes, me and Jason would go visit my mom, wherever she was living, and it never seemed real. It seemed like she was more like my sister, you know? I mean, she acted real young, she looked young. I don't think she really knew how to be a mother herself."

"The bad stuff that happened was because of me and my uncle not getting along sometimes. He'd beat up on me, and I'd run away. The first time I ended up in jail for running, I was eleven. It wasn't like I was being held for a crime or anything, they were just waiting for someone to come and pick me up.

"Another time I ran with my brother Jason. We were unhappy, maybe he'd beat up both of us, I don't remember. He could get real mean, say real bad stuff to us. Anyway, we took off for a day and then just came home. We got spanked when we got home, too, but we just laughed about it. My uncle said, 'Which one of you is going to get it first?' and we just laughed and made a joke of it. I think it made him madder."

"DAMON BETTER BE DIFFERENT THAN ME"

A tall, dark-haired, visibly pregnant woman walks into the room from a back bedroom. She smiles quickly and goes into the kitchen.

"That's Cathy," William explains quickly. "She's my girlfriend. Pregnant again, about six months along. We're still trying to figure out what we're doing—our lives are in kind of a mess right now. I mean, we got Damon, and another one coming by summertime. My heart gets beating faster just thinking about it.

"We're not sure if we're going to get married. I don't know why; I'm not sure it's right or if it's wrong. I been with her a couple of years, since I was seventeen. She's not my first girlfriend or anything—I had a fair amount when I was younger. But she's the one I've cared the most about. And she's the mother of my son." He rolls his eyes. "Sons, I guess. Or daughter and son, whichever it is.

"I'll tell you something. It's changed me around having kids. I used to be in trouble all the time. I'm saying *all the time*. And that's a big part of why I care so much about Damon. I don't want him to turn out like me. Damon better be different than me.

"Every once in a while I think about doing something stupid, like I always done before. But then I think about ending up in jail, and that I'd miss important things, like his walking, or doing things with him for the first time. I like to see him learn new things, new words, how he laughs. He's fifteen months now, Damon is, and I've got a real commitment to him. I don't know about marriage, though. It seems real final. But then I think, 'Man, it's been like two years, and I ain't left her yet.' That's something."

"JAIL WAS PART OF MY GROWING UP"

As if on cue, a little boy in tiny blue jeans and a cowboy shirt comes walking into the room, chattering unintelligibly. William scoops him up and sets him on his knee.

"I care so much about Damon. I don't want him to turn out like me," William says, referring to his tangles with the law as a youth. William stresses that he is trying hard to be a law-abiding citizen and a good father.

"This is Damon," he says proudly. "He's walking, doing everything. He's saying a few little words now—'mama,' 'dada,' 'baba'—but he's learning every day. He's great, aren't you, boy?"

The baby chortles and puts his arms around William, who plants a kiss on the top of his head and puts him down on the floor. Damon finds a blue rubber dog under the coffee table and sits down to investigate it.

"Jail was part of my growing up, too," William continues. "Sometimes it was for getting drunk, sometimes just getting into trouble with a bunch of my friends back when we were young. There was a group of us—I was eleven, and the oldest was fourteen. That was the time when I was living with my mom for a while.

"Me and those guys would drink back then. It wasn't hard to get liquor—grown-ups would sometimes give it to you if you would drink with them, just keeping them company. And my best friend's dad was a bootlegger. He had cases and cases of beer, so he wouldn't notice if there was a twelve-pack or two missing once in a while. Back then, my grandma was mad, she didn't like it that I was getting in trouble living at my mom's. She wanted me in counseling when I was about twelve; she said I had no business drinking. I was just being rebellious, I think. I eventually went back to live with my grandma, 'cause I guess my mom couldn't control me, I don't know."

FOURTEEN OR FIFTEEN FELONIES

By the age of fourteen, William had moved on to more serious crimes, however.

"They were little crimes, little break-ins or something on that line," William remembers. "I don't think it was the money I was doing it for, since my grandma was always willing to give me a little money whenever I asked her. I think it was just for fun, for the thrill. I'd use the money I got for drinking and things like that.

"I can't blame my friends for this stuff, this break-in business. It was just me," he says with a good-natured laugh. "It's funny—you wouldn't think I would be so bad at it that I'd get caught, but I did. Usually a bunch of guys doing stuff draws more attention by neighbors. I must have been real lame at it. So anyhow, they put me on probation, and then after ten arrests, I was put on the criminal list.

"Some of the arrests weren't a problem at all. They'd put me under house arrest sometimes, and that wasn't bad. They gave me a lot of leeway—just had to be home by curfew is all. But it was okay for me to hang around with my friends during the day as long as I let the police know where I was going to be.

"But I don't know," he says with a baffled shrug. "I just seemed to get worse and worse. I was in jail one time, and I pulled a knife on someone. That was when I started into doing some felonies like assaults, aggravated robbery; first-, second-, and third-degree robbery. I was in about a month for that knife thing. I got questioned by detectives and everything. And I just kept getting in trouble, and before long I ended up with fourteen or fifteen felonies.

"And really," he says in a confidential tone, "all these things they call 'felonies' maybe weren't. It's just that after the first one, after you get down with someone, it's an assault. It gets blown out of proportion, even if it's just a real quick fight, nothing major at all."

ON THE RUN

Cathy comes in the room waving a colorful dinosaur bib at Damon, who chortles again and moves quickly toward her. It's lunchtime, and he is hungry. William gives his son a quick pat on the rear end as he passes.

"Just before I was fifteen, I came here from South Dakota. I had messed up with the police there; I had broke the terms of my parole. So they put out a warrant for my arrest. If I'd got caught, they would have me put in jail for seven years! See, I was supposed to be home by curfew—that's 9:00 every night. So then I took off from South Dakota, came up here because I wanted to see my mom.

"For a while, I hid out at the reservation back there; see, the state police got no jurisdiction on an Indian reservation, so they can't arrest nobody. It's like a country all its own. My dad lived on the reservation, and I thought I'd go see him. He was pretty cool. He was in the movie *Thunderheart*, which they filmed on the reservation where he was. After a time there, I left and continued on up here. I cut my hair so nobody would recognize me if I got stopped."

William jumps to his feet and searches a nearby tabletop covered with framed photographs. He finds what he is looking for and holds it up.

"See, this is what I looked like before, with long hair. *Really* long, huh? I look a whole lot different with it short like it is now. I was hoping that if I stayed out of trouble here, then I wouldn't have to worry too much about having my record catch up with me. I hitch-

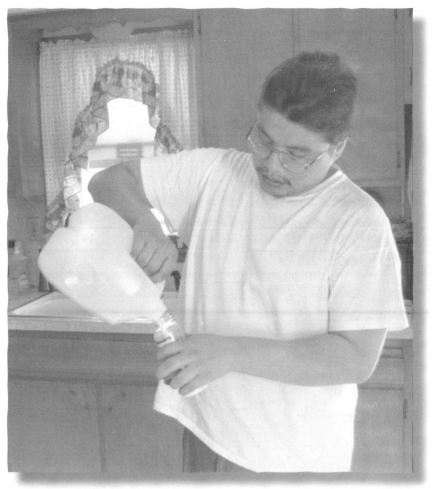

William fills a bottle with milk for his son, Damon. Fatherhood has changed William's life, forcing him to reevaluate his past choices and consider his future plans more carefully.

hiked all the way here. I had the wrong address written down for my mom, so I didn't find her right away. But I sort of knew the general area, so I was riding a bike around and found her car. I got lucky."

"IT WAS STUPID"

But William's luck didn't last long. Although he was going to try to stay out of trouble once he left South Dakota, only a short time later he had committed another felony.

"It was stupid," he says, berating himself. "I had just talked to my probation officer back in South Dakota, told him where I was, and he told me for my own good, don't come back to that state again. And I knew I could handle that. But he also told me not to screw up here, or my record would come back to haunt me, and it sure did.

"I pulled out a gun on some kids; it was a fight over a sweater. It was my sweater, but my ex-girlfriend had it, and I wanted it back. Anyhow, there were these bigger guys that started messing with me, trying to keep me from getting my sweater back. It was stupid, I know that. So yeah, I got charged with a felony.

"My probation officer back there tried to get me extradited, so I could face trial back there. That would have been bad, seven years minimum—I wouldn't have been out until I was twenty-one! But I was lucky, because it turned out that South Dakota's so poor, they don't extradite people.

"They were going to send me to a young offenders' prison just south of here, but it turned out that the minimum age there was fifteen, and I was still fourteen. So all that was left for me was the county home school. That was no big deal, kind of like camp. We got to go outside a lot, go places, play sports. I made lots of friends there. And I was going to treatment for chemical abuse—mostly alcohol and weed [marijuana]—and I was making some friends there, too. It seemed like I hadn't been here very long, and I was getting pretty well connected."

MEETING CATHY

William stayed at the county home school off and on for three years, and it did little to rehabilitate him, nor did he cut down much on his use of marijuana and alcohol.

"If anything," he says, laughing, "I ended up getting more drinking buddies. But there was one good thing about going there. That treatment center was where I met Cathy.

"She was at the center, visiting a guy I'd started talking to—he was her cousin. After a while, we got to kind of talking, too, and we really liked each other. She was a little older than me, but you'd never guess it to look at her. Anyhow, I felt like we were good together almost right away. And we started living together almost right away, too, since I didn't have anywhere else to be. She had a place, and it seemed like I was always over there. She was working at the time—I think she was doing telemarketing or something like that. Just a few months later, she found out she was pregnant. We

William's girlfriend, Cathy, became pregnant shortly after they started dating because they did not use any form of birth control.

hadn't been too good about doing any birth control or anything. Just trying to be lucky, but it didn't work for us."

Cathy did not tell him she was pregnant, for they found out at the same time, he says.

"It was a case where we'd be drinking and stuff," he explains, "and she'd have these weird hangovers the next day—it seemed like they went on forever. She was always throwing up, being sick and acting like she had the flu or something. Well, one of my aunties that lives up here mentioned that she'd felt just like that when she was first pregnant. She said drinking really made her feel rotten.

"So what we did is go and get one of those home pregnancy tests at the drugstore, and it came up positive. There was no doubt about it. So we went to the clinic then, and she had a real exam and everything with the doctor, and she told Cathy and me that she had to stop drinking, because it was bad for the baby—in other words, we were going to be parents."

"IT DON'T REALLY HIT YOU UNTIL LATER"

William claims that he was not scared or nervous when they heard the news.

"It don't really hit you until later, I'm convinced of that," he maintains. "I've talked to a couple other guys, and they say the same thing. I mean, you might feel something, especially if you were really nervous about the idea of having a kid, like if you didn't like the girl or something. But I liked Cathy, and the idea of a kid didn't seem too bad. When I *did* get scared, though, is when she got real pregnant—fat and everything—at about eight months. That's when I started saying to myself, Oh my God, there really is a baby, and it's coming real soon!"

It was not difficult to announce the pregnancy to their families. Cathy's mother was dead, and she had no idea where her father might be.

"A pretty carefree family, I guess," he says. "For me, it was just my mom, because by the time Cathy got pregnant, my dad had died, back on the reservation. Heart attack. Anyhow, Cathy wanted me to tell my mom right away, but I didn't feel comfortable doing that. I don't really know why—it wasn't like she was real strict with me. Like I told you, it was my grandma that raised me, not her. But it ended up okay, because it turned out that my mom could tell about Cathy being pregnant. She says women can tell that stuff real easy about other women, even if they don't know them real well. So she guessed, and it didn't matter at all to her. My grandma, she wasn't upset either. So everything was okay as far as families.

"Marriage was not a real question—at least I don't remember it being brought up then. Me and Cathy were already living together, so we just stayed together. Plus, my life was so messed up with the law and liquor and weed and everything. I spent no time at all thinking about getting someone to marry me. That would have been just great," he jokes. "Have to worry about that, too, being a husband."

"HE'S AMAZING"

Cathy's pregnancy was uncomfortable. She had backaches and was tired much of the time. William remembers that it seemed the time was not passing quickly enough, that her pregnancy went on for years instead of months.

"I got real excited at the end, when she was almost ready to deliver him," he remembers. "We were thinking about names, and

Remembering his girlfriend's pregnancy, William admits, "I did get scared . . . when she got real pregnant—fat and everything—at about eight months. That's when I started saying to myself, Oh my God, there really is a baby, and it's coming real soon!"

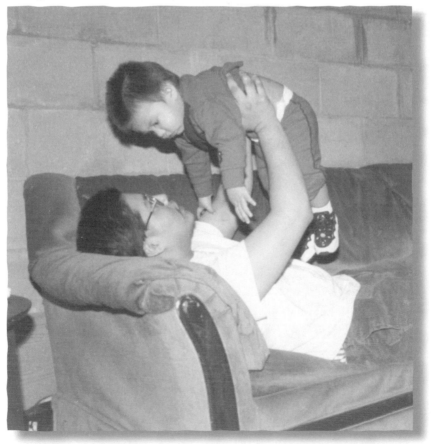

wondering who the baby would look like. Her stomach was so big, and her legs got real swollen, too, so thinking about the baby was about all she had the energy to do.

"We told my mom that if she wanted to name the baby, we'd be honored. But when she did, we didn't like it at all. She wanted Chaska Lloyd or something like that if the baby was a boy—the Chaska part means 'first boy' in Lakota. I don't even remember what her girl name was, to tell you the truth.

"So we were thinking of something ourselves, and Damon popped into our minds. I think maybe it was because of Damon Wayums [Wayans], but I'm not sure. Anyway, my mom wasn't too mad or anything. We weren't trying to disrespect her, we just thought Chaska was wrong. Anyway, I kind of wanted his last name to be the same as mine, and Cathy had no problem with that.

"Anyhow, when he was ready to come into the world, Damon was a hard birth. It was hell for Cathy, real hell. She was in labor for more than twenty-four hours, and she wasn't getting anywhere for a lot of the time, because the baby had turned funny. She was really in rough shape, and the doctors ended up taking the baby by cesarean. That was kind of strange, because having the baby by an operation wasn't even something we had thought about. It makes recuperating real tough.

"But Damon was healthy and strong, right from the start," William smiles. "I remember thinking, 'He's amazing!' He had lots of thick black hair and looked real husky. A good set of lungs, too. I was real proud, and my mom was, too. I remember feeling really kind of humble, you know, like I didn't deserve to have such a beautiful son."

"A BAD HOME FOR A FAMILY"

At the beginning of Damon's life, William had no job but insists he was able to provide for his new family well enough, although to-day he is not at all proud of the manner in which he did so.

"It was not that hard for me," he says. "Little hustles—stealing, shoplifting, and returning the stuff for cash. Selling some weed—that could have been a great career for me, except that I was smoking more than I sold."

He laughs again. "I'm not advocating it, no. In fact, it was my aunties who got me into smoking weed in the first place. It's true! Back when I first came here, when I was fourteen, I'd be over there visiting, and they'd be smoking, getting high constantly. The whole family—the girls steal, and they all get high. All the time, every day. Those aunties were a real bad influence on all the kids in our family. Nobody likes their kids going over there, because it's going to happen.

"But even though it might not have been my fault at first, I sure kept up long after I stopped visiting the aunties," he admits. "Me and Cathy and the baby were living in a real bad part of the city, nothing like this neighborhood at all. It was one of those big brown buildings over by the freeway, you know? You always read in the paper how there was a murder there the night before, always gang stuff. Lots of drive-bys, lots of shoot-outs, lots of guns and shouting and cussing.

"Our place wasn't much better on the inside—a bad home for a family. It was completely mice infested. It seems like they were everywhere; they weren't shy, either. They'd run right across your feet, across your bed. Lots of roaches, too. We'd keep the place clean, but the mice and bugs were in the building, just in the walls. Nothing we could do about that, but it was a bad place to have a baby.

"Anyhow, I was making the rent selling weed, selling a lot of crack. It was the only way I could make good money. And no, Cathy didn't complain at all. Didn't I bring home lots of money? And she liked that. I'm talking $500 or more in a night, easy. No, she wasn't complaining."

"THOUSANDS OF DOLLARS ON NOTHING"

Asked what he spent all of his money on, William shrugs hopelessly.

"I wasn't saving nothing," he says with embarrassment. "I was drinking it up, I spent thousands of dollars on nothing. We'd eat out, go out to eat at Market's and get the best meals. I'm serious, we spent it on nothing. Yeah, we'd buy groceries and lots of milk and formula and stuff. Some clothes and diapers. But God, I wish I could go back to that time and put half of that money aside and save it. Jeez, I could use it now—we could put a down payment on a place to live!"

William says that his drug business continued to thrive until a new gang moved into the neighborhood. Their presence, and the frightening events that followed, is the reason they came to live for a little while at his mother's.

"I was doing good, selling mostly little twenty rocks of crack," he says. "I just carried the stuff in little bags in my mouth. That way, if the police came by, I could either swallow it, or dash inside the building and dump it. It was a perfect location, and business was booming. And the cops weren't going after nobody. Hell, I could just run right up to cars that came by, and make my deals.

"But then these guys—the Detroit Boys—moved in. They told me it was their building, and I had no business doing my dealing there. They told me I had to pay them a fee on what I was making, since they claimed the territory. But I wasn't doing that. I wasn't going to pay them anything, and since I was using up the money so fast, I *couldn't* have given them anything, you know? So then it got real bad for us for a while. Those guys were looking for me, and they threatened that they were going to get their money or else."

AFRAID FOR CATHY, AFRAID FOR DAMON

William says it was the scariest time of his life, worrying about being killed by the Detroit Boys and worrying about the danger to Cathy and Damon.

"I had my gun, my sawed-off shotgun, right by the bed. It was on the floor, by the side of the bed where I slept. I always tried to sleep with my hand over the side, so I could wake up and grab it quick if I needed it. We had our bed right by the door. Cathy would say, 'That's bad in your own house when you can't even sleep, you're always scared.'

"She was right, too," William agrees. "I was always paranoid, always listening for the sound of them in the hall. I'd hear them outside, too. I looked out the window half the day, just to see who was coming in or out. I'd hide when they came upstairs and knocked on the door.

"At first, they were kind of nice to Cathy and Damon. They'd ask where I was, and she'd lie and say I was out. They'd be talking to little Damon, calling him 'my man' and stuff like that. But after a while, they were threatening.

"They'd just hang out waiting for me sometimes, just sitting on the steps by the building, smoking weed. They started telling everyone in our building to be looking for me, that they were going to shoot me in the head if I didn't pay them. They even said they'd give a few hundred bucks to anyone who'd help them find me. It was all about revenge, all about teaching me a lesson. I mean, they were willing to spend more on reward money than I even owed them! They weren't messing around," William says, shuddering a little. "I knew I was—and maybe even Damon and Cathy—going to wind up dead if we didn't get out of there pretty soon."

"I Learned a Lesson from That"

William says that he still worries that the Detroit Boys will find him, even though his mother's house is several miles from the building in which they used to live.

William regrets that he worked as a drug dealer to support his family and hopes he can make a clean break. "I don't want to be bad no more, I really don't," he explains.

"I hear a car outside, and I'm crouching by the window," he says sheepishly. "I've got my gut in a knot half the time, worrying about it. It was so scary. But I learned a lesson from that. In fact, I learned a few lessons.

"First of all, I learned to keep your home and your business very separate. You don't want people coming to your house. Because if they can't find me, they may be willing to hurt my family. So I was endangering Cathy and the kid. And that's real shameful.

"That's the rest of the lesson I learned," he continues. "I don't want to be bad no more, I really don't. I been in trouble so much in my life. I been robbing people, stealing their goods. I been having fights, drawing guns, just being the kind of person I am. But I don't want to be that person no more.

"See, I got to think about Damon. I mean, it's more than just the fear of him getting hurt because of me. It's me, too, getting into stupid stuff again, just because I can't control my temper or whatever. He'll be growing up and I don't want to be in some jail somewhere. And then when I get out, he wouldn't remember me, or maybe Cathy would marry somebody else, and Damon would think of that guy as daddy. Plus, I wouldn't want him being ashamed of me. I don't want to miss all the good stuff that's coming with him, and with this next little baby. I mean, if that's the whole reason I have for living, if I can't change for Damon, I might as well give up."

"I Want Damon to Have a Home"

The possibility that his son might someday be ashamed of him is almost too frightening for William to talk about.

"I'll tell you something," he confesses. "You know how I told you we gave him my last name? Well, I was even tempted for a while to make him William, too, just like me. I didn't, and you want to know the whole reason why not? I kept thinking, What if I end up in jail, or what if I slip back into the stuff I used to do, and screw up real bad? Do I want that kid growing up mad at his father for giving him the same name? That was the biggest fear I had. So I couldn't give him my first name, too. It made me feel bad, like real envious of guys who can think about naming their sons the same name, and put a Junior after it. They don't even have to worry about the kid resenting it later on.

"I want him to have a real home, too. I want to get out of my mom's house soon. Partly because I don't get along with her boyfriend. He's mean, and he doesn't like having us around. I've gotten into fights with him, beat him up a couple of times. He gets drunk, see, and he says some stupid stuff about me. And plus, he brings up mistakes I've made, bad stuff that happened before.

"But mostly I want Damon to have a home so we can be together," he continues. "Cathy will be staying home full-time with the kids. I want to get us a place that's nicer. Even staying at one of the motels down the street—get a place for two weeks at a time, so I can pay for it every time I get a paycheck. At least we'd be on our own, no other people living with us."

GETTING OFF WELFARE

Although William is grateful for the welfare programs that have helped Cathy and Damon, he says he sometimes feels guilty accepting the money.

Taking a break from his interview, William changes Damon's diaper. Although he is grateful to his mother for letting him and his family live with her, he hopes he and Cathy will be able to afford an apartment of their own soon.

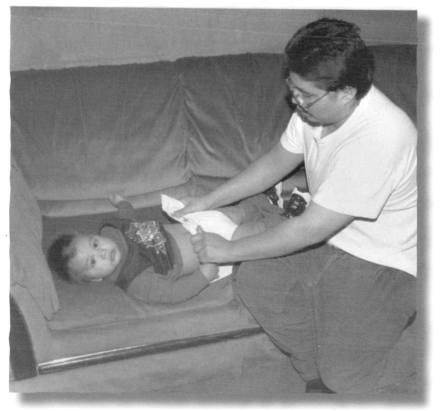

"We get free formula from WIC, and Cathy's in this county program that helps single mothers get education, get free child care while she's in school. I know that's great for her, and I'm glad, because she'll have a lot more choices when she wants to work. But I ain't on my own, I'm not standing on my two feet neither. I got to be fighting this battle every single day, so I don't do something stupid, like rob someone, sell more drugs. It's like knowing there's a whole lot of money under that rock over there, but you know it's wrong to lift up the rock.

"But I want Damon to have a room of his own, some toys or clothes that haven't been owned by a hundred other kids already, you know? Anyway, the biggest thing for me to do as a father is fight this uphill battle every day, stop thinking about easy money. So when I'm making honest money, even if it's a lot less than if I was dealing, I'll be happier about it."

BETTER FRIENDS, TOO

William says he will be happy, too, if Damon has more sense than he himself had about his choice of friends.

"I don't even want my kids knowing any of the guys I know," he says with his jaw clenched. "Just start out clean, a clean slate. I don't even like my younger brother Jason knowing those guys! I'm not just talking about the Detroit Boys, but even the kind of guys I was friends with in treatment, or in the county home school.

"One guy got me with a razor blade on the bus downtown a few months ago. He had heard this rumor that I'd been paid $10,000 by the cops to tell that these guys I know killed a guy. They *did* kill a guy, but I didn't tell no cops, so the rumor wasn't true. But they're willing to slice me up on the bus, just because they heard something.

"Those were *bad* guys, those guys that did the killing. They killed a young guy at Subway, out in the suburbs. They found blood on one of these guy's pants, so they had him, and they got the other one that did it, too. I feel so lucky that I didn't get involved in that, because the fact is that I *was* supposed to go out with those guys that night. That would have been me getting arrested, too, just for being there, and that would have been life for me. What happened was I got sick drinking that day, something that *never* happens to me. So I was home, and that saved my life, saved my life with Damon and Cathy."

"Yeah," he says, thinking about it, "it's a real important thing to get good friends in life. I'm hoping Damon can make lots better choices about guys than I have."

"I'd Have Had Him Later"

Asked if he regrets having a child so early in his life, William nods almost imperceptibly.

"Yeah, I'd have had him later. I don't want to wish him away, but if I could have him exactly the way he is, and nothing would have changed about him, I wish we could have waited to have a baby. I want a full-time job, so I can do better. I want to be able to get that dealing stuff behind me, that stuff with the Detroit Boys, so I can walk around during the day outside, showing my face, not being so scared.

"I'm wishing Cathy hadn't gotten pregnant this second time, too. And we were trying to be careful, she was taking these Depo Provera shots but her hair started falling out and she couldn't lose no weight from her other pregnancy. Bad side effects, yeah. So— she got pregnant. We found out the same way as before—getting sick after she'd been drinking and stuff."

William looks a bit uncomfortable when asked if he thinks he and Cathy will stay together.

"I can't honestly say. I mean, I hope so, but there's all these prob- lems right now. We ain't getting along real good. We yell a lot, have lots of arguments. I've thought about how it would be if we split up, and we've talked about it a couple of times. But we've been able to get everything sorted out so far. Who knows what will happen, though? I know I don't ever want to be away from Damon. He's the only reason I got to be a good person. I don't want to lose him."

"No Guy Can Understand Unless He's Been There"

William says that before Damon, he would never have believed a person could feel so important, so happy, or so loved.

"It's nothing you can explain, not really," he says happily. "But no guy can understand unless he's been there, been a father for the first time. It's just such a great feeling, looking at him, watching him grow a little each day.

"It's so much fun to have him around—he's a good baby. Play- ing with him is fun; he likes to wrestle with me. He laughs so hard!

Despite the happiness his son has brought into his life, William regrets having a child at such an early age.

He likes to play with the ball, likes to toss it back and forth to me. I'm really waiting for the weather to turn, so we can go outside. He'll love that."

William leans forward, as though he is going to share something confidential.

"You know, the best thing is when I'm just lying around, just on the floor, and he'll come walking up and bend down and kiss me. That's such a great feeling, probably my favorite part of being a father so far. And another one is when he's trying to sleep, but he doesn't quite fall asleep unless he's lying right by you, touching you somehow. He's a kid who really likes contact—maybe I do too. And I've been away a couple of times, and, boy, Cathy says he misses me then. But I tell her how much I missed him. It sounds like it's pretty equal. I'm always in a hurry to get home, just to see him."

TRYING TO HOLD ON

William says he knows that a lot of what is troubling him now is the incident with the Detroit Boys, and the danger they may pose for him and his family.

"Once I know I can stop worrying about them, I think we'll all be happier," he admits. "I know my problem now is stress. I smoke weed, drink a little—that's not for partying, that's just to relieve the tension I feel. It's paranoia sometimes, big time. I've been thinking lately that I should go to the hospital and get some pills or something that could settle me down. I don't want to be nervous and strung out like this all the time. I expect the worst, and my imagination goes wild. I wake up every morning scared, and that's how I go to sleep every night, too.

"I don't have a gun anymore. I'd like to be able to say that it's because of Damon being able to walk now, so he don't get into finding it and firing it by mistake. But the truth is, I got broke and had to sell it. But really, I don't want a gun, because I know I'd use it. Best not to put it in my reach, same as weed.

"Cathy thinks I need to calm down, and that would stop our fighting, too. Just calm down, like she says. I think if I can find a job—maybe two part-time jobs—I'll have one less thing to worry about. Right now I'm just showing up a couple days a week at the temporary agency, getting little cash jobs like vacuuming carpeting, stuff like that. But on Monday, I find out if I got these little part-timers I applied for. And I got options at the big mall, too. They got this computer that you can put your name in, your age, your experience. And it automatically goes through and flags the stores that are hiring and sends applications to you. There's choices, yeah, so I'm hoping I get something fast. And it'll take my mind off my other worries, at the same time."

Epilogue

In the months since these four young men were interviewed for this book, some significant changes have occurred in their lives.

Jason—along with Jessica and Tyler—are now living with his parents, but he would like to find them a place of their own. However, for the time being, things are fine at home—just a little crowded, he says.

Jamie has had trouble getting along with his girlfriend. They have split up, and he does not see as much of his daughter. He is still working as a custodian at his church and is playing football for his high school. Jamie is seeing another girl, but he maintains that he is "not going to get serious this time."

William and Kathy have had their baby—another little boy. William is working part-time at the mall, but he is looking for a full-time position that would give him insurance benefits.

Brad is still hanging out with his friends, playing football, and skateboarding. He and Kim do not see one another, and he says he has not seen Jordan for almost two months. He seems resigned to the fact that he is not going to play much of a role in his daughter's life, at least for now. He still has no job but is considering joining the air force.

Ways You Can Get Involved

THE FOLLOWING ORGANIZATIONS CAN BE
CONTACTED FOR MORE INFORMATION ABOUT
TEEN FATHERS.

Alan Guttmacher Institute
111 Fifth Ave.
New York, NY 10003

Works to develop family planning programs through research and
public education.

Institute for Responsible Fatherhood and Family Revitalization
1146 19th St. NW, Suite 800
Washington, DC 20036

This nonprofit organization helps reunite fathers with their children and provides counseling and family outreach support.

MELD for Young Dads
123 N. 3rd St., Suite 507
Minneapolis, MN 55401

Provides education and support for teen fathers who want to become more active in their children's lives. Offers career help, child
health and development classes, and stress relief.

National Center on Fathers and Families
Graduate School of Education
University of Pennsylvania
3700 Walnut St., Box 58
Philadelphia, PA 19104

The center facilitates the effective involvement of fathers through policy research, program development, and information dissemination.

Planned Parenthood
810 Seventh Ave.
New York, NY 10019

Provides counseling about contraceptives and reproductive services through clinics around the United States.

For Further Reading

Joy G. Dryfoos, *Putting Boys in the Picture: A Review of Programs to Promote Sexual Responsibility Among Young Males*. Santa Cruz, CA: Network Publications, 1988. Good references, helpful list of organizations and programs that can help young fathers.

Karen Gravelle and Leslie Peterson, *Teenage Fathers*. New York: Julian Messner, 1992. Interviews with teenagers who have fathered children.

Earl Ofari Hutchinson, *Black Fatherhood: The Guide to Male Parenting*. Los Angeles: Middle Passage, 1995. Although not geared especially for teenage fathers, this book does provide good, readable information about the history of black fathers in the United States, from the era of slavery to the 1990s.

Jeanne Warren Lindsay, *Teen Dads: Rights, Responsibilities, and Joys*. Buena Park, CA: Morning Glory Press, 1993. An easy-to-understand guidebook written especially for teen fathers. Helpful information on baby care; good bibliography.

———, *Teenage Marriage: Coping with Reality*. Buena Park, CA: Morning Glory Press, 1988. Frank talk focusing on the responsibilities and difficulties as well as joys faced by teenagers who decide to get married.

Kyle D. Pruett, *The Nurturing Father*. New York: Warner Books, 1987. Moderately difficult reading, but good information on the importance of a father in children's lives.

Index

ABOUT THE AUTHOR

Gail B. Stewart is the author of more than eighty books for children and young adults. She lives in Minneapolis, Minnesota, with her husband, Carl, and their sons, Ted, Elliot, and Flynn. When she is not writing, she spends her time reading, walking, and watching her sons play soccer.

Although she has enjoyed working on each of her books, she says that *The Other America* series has been especially gratifying. "So many of my past books have involved extensive research," she says, "but most of it has been library work—journals, magazines, books. But for these books, the main research has been very human. Spending the day with a little girl who has AIDS, or having lunch in a soup kitchen with a homeless man—these kinds of things give you insight that a library alone just can't match."

Stewart hopes that readers of this series will experience some of the same insights—perhaps even being motivated to use some of the suggestions at the end of each book to become involved with someone of the Other America.

ABOUT THE PHOTOGRAPHER

Twenty-two-year-old Theodore E. Roseen currently attends Hamline University in St. Paul, Minnesota, and is studying secondary education in social studies. He has been a photographer for the university's student newspaper, *The Oracle*, for more than three years.